WHEN THE VOW BREAKS

Portraits of Divorce Involving a Private Investigator

by

M. Duane Adair

Bloomington, IN

authorHOUSE®

Milton Keynes, UK

AuthorHouse™
1663 Liberty Drive, Suite 200
Bloomington, IN 47403
www.authorhouse.com
Phone: 1-800-839-8640

AuthorHouse™ UK Ltd.
500 Avebury Boulevard
Central Milton Keynes, MK9 2BE
www.authorhouse.co.uk
Phone: 08001974150

First published by AuthorHouse 1/10/2007

ISBN: 1-4208-6541-2 (sc)
ISBN: 1-4208-6540-4 (dj)

Printed in the United States of America
Bloomington, Indiana

This book is printed on acid-free paper.

Contents

Acknowledgements

The writing of this book would not have been accomplished without the help, encouragement and support of others. We gratefully acknowledge our clients whose *real-life* stories are both the foundation and motivation of this book. We thank you for your confidence in using our agency. We also appreciate the collaborative affiliation with the various first-class attorneys with whom we work and for their referrals.

Introduction

If you are reading this book, chances are you are considering hiring a private investigator (PI). If you are considering hiring a PI, more than likely you are one of the fifty percent of Americans contemplating divorce. Unfortunately, divorce is the number one reason our services are retained and because of the numerous divorce-related cases we have dealt with over the past three decades, sharing this information is the primary reason for writing this book.

My goal is to explain the role of a private investigator in the two most common types of cases seen in our office – Divorce and Child Custody. The tools used to gather information for these cases and the importance of choosing an attorney who knows how to use information will be discussed as well as other reasons for hiring a PI. Although the bulk of our business stems from divorce-related circumstances, we do not promote divorce and would encourage anyone contemplating divorce to exhaust all possible avenues before throwing in the towel, especially when minor children are involved. However, we do not condone abuse and would never encourage anyone to stay in an abusive situation. By and large, when a person has reached the point of hiring a private investigator, the marriage is frequently beyond repair.

Throughout this book you will notice "cases" frequently referenced. At the root of each "case" is a **human being** and we have built our business by never forgetting this. It is easy for a good investigator to live and breathe this profession and derive a great deal of satisfaction from the actual work however, the greatest reward comes from working with and serving our clients.

This book does not replace or override legal advice from a competent attorney. All comments or suggestions should be considered only as comments not as legal advice. You should consult with your attorney *prior* to doing *anything* about which you are not certain.

This book should serve *only* as a guide *(although not comprehensive)* to planning and to make you aware of precautions one might take when contemplating divorce or if you believe you may become the target of divorce. This book will help you to better understand the business of a private investigator and how their services will aid your case. It will also give you guidelines to follow when choosing an investigator to fit the needs of your case, as well as helping you to feel more comfortable in your search for the truth.

One

The Business of Private Investigation

A well heeled, smartly dressed blonde beauty stood tall in a discreet, yet well appointed office, lifting her blouse exposing lingerie Victoria tries to keep secret. The skilled private investigator stood poised, a quarter of a century of experience reflected in his demeanor, quietly mirroring the upper echelon image of the woman standing before him. Deftly, he slipped the small recording device into the constraints of the powder pink lacy garment, with the precision and detachment of a seasoned surgeon.

Due to such noted detective writers as Raymond Chandler and Mickey Spillane, most people expect the private investigation business to be "glamorous" -- the booze, blondes, and blinking neon signs type of glamour. There are some moments in which one feels he has perhaps walked out of the pages of one of those novels, as the previous excerpt describes. However, the work leading up to those moments is far from glamorous.

Throughout the pages of this book you will become acquainted with the work of a real-life private investigator. Although the public has this Hollywood idea of a private investigator, our profession is rooted in the mid-eighteen hundreds chasing train robbers while working as detectives for the railroads.

Allen Pinkerton, a former barrel maker from Scotland, founded the Pinkerton National Detective Agency in 1850, the nation's oldest agency. Pinkerton is known as the first "Private Eye." In fact, the logo for his agency, a single open eye with the motto, "*We Never Sleep*," actually serves as the root of the term "Private Eye." Pinkerton's agency is responsible for preventing an assassination attempt on Abraham Lincoln, organizing the first Secret Service during the War Between the States, and serving as a model for the formation of the Federal Bureau of Investigation. Pinkerton's agents set the pace for the stylized detective genre. "Pinkerton's Code" was one of utmost honesty and integrity.1

Technology in the 21st Century has made the work of a detective much easier, but certain aspects of the work remain the same. Finding and researching information and following the proverbial trail of evidence are examples of this.

A favorite story to illustrate this dates back to 1883 and involves a handkerchief. A stagecoach robber, dubbed Black Bart, eluded the law for almost ten years before leaving behind a clue at what would become his final holdup.

A simple handkerchief was found bearing the mark of a San Francisco laundry. This one small clue led to the breaking of this case, but only after contact was made with each one of the approximately ninety-one laundry houses in San Francisco.2 Finding the handkerchief is one of those "*moments*" spoken of earlier. Often, a lot of time is invested for a few moments of information, but those few moments can break a case wide open. Those pieces of information are what the client is paying for, and is why hiring a first-class detective is so important.

Before continuing, let us back up a bit and consider this question: *"To hire a private investigator or not to hire a private investigator?"* You may be asking yourself: *"Is a PI really necessary?"* or *"Is this something I can do myself?"* Let us deal with the last question first and the answer to the first question may become evident.

While the dilemma of hiring an investigator pales in comparison to the predicament in your life, it is valid. If you need to know the truth about your marriage, your relationship or any other situation in which you find yourself, investigating the situation yourself is certainly not recommended. There are three major risks involved – objectivity, discovery and credibility.

One obvious risk is your emotional involvement in the case. It is impossible to be objective when gathering information about your own life considering the affect it may have on your emotional stability and your future. Hiring an objective third party to investigate these matters will be in your favor.

You are free to go through your days as normally as possible and allow the detective to gather information to either prove or disprove your suspicions. Your emotional attachment to the subject of an investigation puts you at risk for being discovered, resulting in a confrontation between yourself and the other party.

A PI will recommend you to go about your daily life, as if nothing out of the ordinary is going on, so as not to tip off the subject. When investigating a loved one and seeing discrepancies, betrayals and suspicious behavior on a daily basis, you would have to have a heart of ice to hide the discoveries made. The hurt and anger you may feel could push you to a confrontation you may regret. If it turns out your significant other is innocent *(innocent until proven guilty)*, you gain peace of mind without risking further mistrust due to being discovered.

If your significant other is cheating and a divorce becomes inevitable, it will be to your advantage to have as much credible information as you possibly can. Therefore, any investigation into the activities of your cheating spouse should remain secret, if you plan to use it later.

Being discreet may not be an easy task if you are observing behavior that contradicts your marital vows. Many different scenarios could transpire if your spouse discovers he or she is being investigated. Always avoid doing anything that would nullify the information gathered or spoil the outcome of your litigation. The risk you take when you put valuable time and effort into your own investigation may be the issue of credibility and admissibility in court. Common sense tells you your testimony in court will be considered prejudiced. It becomes a matter of HE SAID/SHE SAID and finding a judge that will tolerate this banter is unlikely.

Think about it. You get on the witness stand and start singing about your soon to be ex-spouse's dirty laundry, then the other party does the same. If this is a custody battle, the court might become so exhausted by such behavior that in the best interest of the children, the Court may decide to place the children with the Department of Human Services. At any rate, it is highly probable that information presented from your own investigation may not be as credible in court. This is another argument for hiring a non-biased, third party to perform the investigation. You may do some very preliminary research yourself to determine if you are the subject of an overactive imagination, or if you are, in fact, the victim of a crime of the heart.

Our agency reluctantly accepted a case that illustrates an overactive imagination. There are many areas in which distrust can breed within a marital relationship. I have learned a great deal about human behavior over the years, but because I am not a counselor I will just relate the story and let you draw your own conclusions.

The receptionist answered the ringing phone to hear a hushed voice nervously requesting to speak to an investigator. After a brief conversation, we arranged to meet in an out-of-the-way diner. The silver haired lady, attempting to disguise herself in a pair of sunglasses, sat conspicuously in a torn red leather chair at a Formica table in the back of the diner. I knew immediately she was my prospective client. We exchanged introductions and she began telling me her story.

Her husband, in his late seventies and retired, is cheating on her. She is completely convinced of it. She explained her suspicions including her information leading to her conclusions.

On occasion, her husband would leave the house stating that he was going to make a purchase at a nearby convenience store. She had made the trip to the convenience store many times and knew it should take no more than eleven minutes, but it was taking him up to twenty-one minutes. So obviously, to her, something suspicious was going on. Additionally, he would leave the house relatively early in the morning and not return until early evening. Knowing her spouse had some type of menial job at a local golf course, she was completely convinced he must be having an affair with one of the several *"college-age"* females working part-time at the golf course.

I accepted the case and continued periodic meetings with the client in secret little out of the way places. I began surveillance and very easily established a consistent routine with the subject. True to her story, he would leave the house by eight o'clock each morning and drive to a coffee shop where he drank coffee, smoked and swapped stories with a regular gang of men similar in age to our subject. From the coffee shop, he would go directly to the golf course, routinely arriving at 10:30 a.m. and spend the day performing his menial duties. This allowed him to spend time outdoors in an environment he obviously loved. He routinely returned home around 5:30 in the evening, just as the client had described.

During the entire five weeks of surveillance the subject's routine varied only on Tuesdays and Fridays when he would drive to the convenience store and buy four packages of Salem Ultra Light 100's cigarettes. Usually on one of these excursions he would also fill his vehicle with gas. I reported his activities to the client every few days. My client was still not convinced all was on the up and up, so she retained my services for a while longer. From my perspective, the subject was taking a mini-vacation each day doing what he enjoyed doing; maybe the client was doing the same thing in her own way – escaping the humdrum routine of her day by disguising her identity and meeting me in secretive locations she wouldn't dare visit without dark sunglasses.

After five weeks of surveillance, photographs and documentation, she finally accepted our findings. The facts proved that her husband was not having an affair. Now, nine years later, they are still married and her spouse never knew he was under investigation because of his wife's suspicions.

This turned out to be a case of an overactive imagination. The client was able to lay her suspicions to rest and find closure without causing unnecessary damage to her marriage. Unfortunately, cases of this type are few and far between. Usually a client's suspicions prove to be much more than an overactive imagination.

The answer to the question -- "Is a PI really necessary?" -- should be obvious. Now that you are aware of the importance of hiring a PI and have determined you need the services of a private investigator, let us discuss the selection criteria.

HOW DO YOU DETERMINE WHICH PI TO HIRE?

According to the Bureau of Labor Statistics, 48,000 jobs were held by private investigators in 2002. By the year 2012, employment in this industry is expected to increase by twenty-one to thirty-five percent.3 The investigation business being one of the fastest growing fields in the country and with thousands of investigators and agencies nationwide, how do you determine which PI to hire?

In our opinion, the best way to find a reputable investigator is by referral from your attorney or a friend who has used an investigator and received satisfactory results. Once you have the name of an investigator, your work is half complete, now you can consider important criteria such as credentials, character, credibility and reputation.

REFERRALS

"Word of Mouth" is the best method of advertising for an investigative agency; it is also an excellent shopping tool, especially when you are looking for an investigator. The majority of my clients are referred by someone who has previously used our agency or one of the attorneys, for whom I regularly work.

If you are consulting with an attorney, ask them for a referral if they have not already recommended one. (The attorney/PI relationship is discussed further in Chapter Seven.) If you know someone who has used a private investigator in the past, find out if the nature of their investigation was similar to yours and ask for the name of the investigator used. The nature of the business is private, so do not to advertise you are looking for a private investigator. Discretely shopping around will be to your advantage.

An interesting referral came my way several years ago. It is interesting because the potential client, John, turned out to be the subject of a prior investigation *(you will be reading the case story later in this chapter)*. John's wife had hired me to investigate his activities, which confirmed he was involved in an extramarital affair. The case ended, but their marriage did not. I was quite surprised when two years later, John inquired about our agency doing an investigation into the activities of his paramour. Apparently, John's affair had continued through the years and now he had become suspicious of his girlfriend's activities.

John stated he had two good reasons for wanting to retain my services. First, he thought it would be cheaper since I already had knowledge and documentation about his girlfriend from his wife's case. Secondly, he told me, "According to my wife, you caught me!" which heightened my credentials in John's eyes.

Of course I did not accept the case, considering this would be a conflict of interest. I advised John we were not taking any new cases at this time; however, he could check back with us in six to seven months.

The entire ordeal was one of those head-shaking moments that caused me to chuckle. It also provided another interesting story to add to the many already filed away in my mind.

Through one source or another, you have found your way to a private investigator. Now is the time to find out if you are about to embark on a "beautiful friendship," as Bogart's famous last line in Casablanca goes. Whether the investigator was a referral or the result of a yellow page search, you still have to decide if the investigator is compatible with your particular case. Most importantly, consider the investigator's honesty, credibility and experience. These qualities must be established to your satisfaction.

CREDENTIALS, CHARACTER, CREDIBILITY AND REPUTATION

A fundamental aspect of the private investigator's credentials is licensing. The majority of the states and the District of Columbia require private investigators to be licensed. Requirements vary from minimal to stringent, depending on the state. Licensure can be verified by contacting your County Clerk of Courts office or the state agency responsible for licensing. For example, in the State of Oklahoma, the Council on Law Enforcement Education and Training *(commonly referred to as C.L.E.E.T.)*, a state agency, issues the license. They also mandate the training required prior to issuing a license, the bonding requirements and the continuing education to maintain the PI's license in good standing.

If you are in a state that does not require licensing, it does not necessarily mean there are no good and/or reputable PIs in your area. However, you would be well advised to get a few references and contact them prior to retaining an investigator.

Complaints, if any, can usually be verified through the licensing board and the Better Business Bureau. Most reputable investigators will be happy to furnish you with references. They should also be members of both local and national professional PI organizations. As in any business, especially when retaining an attorney or private investigator, credibility, character and reputation can become key factors in the outcome of your case.

Credibility of the private investigator may make the difference whether the court will believe the information or not. A significant consideration should be the degree to which the investigator is experienced in *testifying before* the court. Many investigators have little or no experience in this very important area. Your attorney will insist the investigator come across as being very poised, confident and credible, when testifying as a witness in your case. The investigator must be prepared and qualified for stringent cross-examination by the opposing attorney, thus increasing the credibility of the information put together for your case. A PI who is unprepared for your trial can be an embarrassment to you, as well as, your attorney. In addition, attempt to scrutinize the overall character and reputation of the PI you retain. Make certain the court will readily accept the investigator's testimony as the truth, backed up by the PI's reliable reputation and scrupulous character in the community.

EXPERIENCE AND BACKGROUND

You will find many investigators come from a criminal justice background. Many enter the field after serving in law enforcement, the military, government auditing and investigative positions, or federal intelligence jobs. I worked for the Federal Bureau of Investigation *(FBI)* and spent some time in the oil industry before beginning my career as a private investigator. The cross over into private investigation from one of the above-mentioned fields is a natural one. However, background only does not insure the success or credibility of an investigator. Many good investigators come from all walks of life. Having been in the business for more than twenty-five years, I can assure you I would not be in business today if I were not excellent at what I do. Overall experience is not the only criteria you should look for, but experience specific to your needs should be on the top of your list.

RATES

The rate is obviously significant, but should not be the determining factor in your search for an investigator. You will find an assortment of rates. As with attorneys, investigators' hourly rates are usually based on their credibility, competency, length of time in the business and success ratio.

Most investigators will require a retainer fee prior to beginning an investigation. You should make every effort to hire the best possible investigator you can find, providing the PI's credentials and expertise match your needs. "You get what you pay for" applies to hiring your attorney as well as your private investigator. If you choose your attorney or PI based on the fee alone, you may be very disappointed. A competent attorney or private investigator will most likely not be the least expensive, however may be less expensive in the long run. You pay for their experience, contacts, database access, professionalism and overall track record handling cases similar to yours.

In the end, you will get what you pay for. Hire a thorough, competent attorney and investigator and you will not be sorry. On numerous occasions, a client has come to us after a fruitless or negative experience with a less than reputable investigator. They have attempted to get by inexpensively, but in the end they have paid double, or more. A credible and reputable investigator will be more than worth the expense and may very well pay for itself by leading to a successful settlement of your case.

Most investigators charge an hourly rate for each man-hour, as well as expenses for things such as mileage, travel expense, telephone calls, copies, etc. This will be discussed with you during the initial consultation. Depending on your case, it may be acceptable to request a cap be set on the fees and expenses, but understand there is no guarantee a limited investigation will produce the information you need. Based on an investigator's experience, it may be possible he or she can give you some sort of estimate, but it can be a little premature because each case has its own set of challenges. Your ultimate total expenditure depends on countless factors such as *location, subject's paranoia, access to "hidden assets," reliability of subject's available records, subject's success in attempting to hide assets and/or a paramour(s), difficulty of the investigation, the number of investigators assigned and many other determining factors.*

A private investigator's knowledge, experience and time are his products just as it is with other service industries, such as electricians, automotive mechanics or attorneys, who provide a needed service with competitive rates. A competent investigator's products may very well resolve a case, find a key witness, catch a cheating spouse, or uncover other unknown factors which could have an impact on you and your children. Do not bargain shop for such a necessary and essential service.

Our firm invests thousands of dollars every year on state-of-the-art equipment, training seminars, proprietary databases, along with continuing education, in an effort to offer our clients the best possible outcome. Make sure the services being offered are comparable, not just cheaper. The experience of interviewing different investigators will help you get a feel for their professionalism, maturity and compatibility with you, the client. The comparison process can yield significant results and is just as important as shopping around for a doctor, attorney, home mortgage or other important decisions you make.

WHAT TO EXPECT AFTER CHOOSING A PI

At this point, let's assume you have successfully matched your needs and bank account to an investigator you feel comfortable with, now what happens?

Once you find a private investigator, request references. Most private investigators will be pleased to provide you with numerous references from colleagues or attorneys with whom they work. They may even provide you with references from previous clients, after first receiving the former client's permission. We protect the identities of our clients and never reveal a client's identity without the client's prior consent.

Should you contact our agency, be prepared for a comprehensive interview before your case is accepted. When a competent attorney has not referred the potential client, it is standard procedure to pre-screen that client during the preliminary stages of the investigation. We consider a face-to-face interview necessary, to evaluate and determine the client's motive and his or her emotional ability to handle the information we obtain during the investigation. However, the majority of the interview will be focused on the specifics of the investigation.

During the initial consultation, which is conducted by the investigator who will be working the case, a number of questions will be asked, some of which might seem insignificant, but clues come in many different forms and fashions, so no detail is too small. You will be asked to provide detailed information regarding your knowledge of the subject(s) and to provide, if easily available, photographs, automobile license tag numbers, places frequented by the subject and suspected paramours.

In our office, we actually begin the preliminary stages of your case, once you have scheduled your initial consultation. Before considering a case, the investigator needs to have as much information as possible on all parties involved, including the client. Due to the nature of the business, the investigator likes to know with whom he is dealing, prior to scheduling a meeting. Therefore, when the client arrives for a consultation, a preliminary or basic plan of action may have already been discussed with the staff. The client will be charged at our standard hourly rate for this initial meeting and interview if he or she does not retain our services.

RETAINING YOUR PI

The next step is to actually retain the services of the investigator. Be prepared to pay the retainer fee at the time an employment agreement is signed, engaging the services of the private investigator. This is the customary procedure for almost every PI, in order to insure adequate funds are available, to conduct a useful investigation. Reputable PI's fees are not inexpensive and are based on having learned what it takes financially to do justice to a case.

The employment agreement may differ from agency to agency, but should contain information such as, but not limited to, the services requested of the PI by the client, a description of costs and fees the client will incur, the retainer amount being paid and the rate for each man hour. Depending upon the type of investigation, the employment agreement may vary to include specific and appropriate language.

For example, the agreement for locating a biological parent will differ slightly from an agreement to investigate an employee. A general employment contract is used for most investigations. These agreements are legally binding and will commence the investigation process.

Once the employment agreement is signed, the client can be assured that someone will be watching out for his or her best interest. The investigators go to work almost immediately on the case, using every resource available to them. Each agency conducts business in its own way, but most reputable agencies will include these certain procedures and elements.

THE OFFICE AND STAFF

The private investigating agency's office and staff are visible criterion, which is simple for the client to evaluate. The size and activity of the staff, as well as the appearance of the actual office, tells a story of its own. I entered the world of private investigation as a one-man agency, which means I did the research, billing, presentations, basic clerical and secretarial duties, and every other task known to a small business, as well as, the investigating. Today I maintain a fully staffed office that provides efficient and timely support to all of the investigators in the field. Everyone in the agency is involved in the entire investigation, with each of the staff having very specific jobs. This allows the investigation to progress smoothly and simultaneously on many different levels, such as research and documentation, as well as investigative work in the field. The support staff in our office is responsible for research and billing, photograph and video documentation, data recovery from proprietary databases, report preparation and a host of other duties generated during each step of the investigation.

A client file is created on the day the employment agreement is signed with our agency. From that day forward, all research material and documentation, relative to the client's case, is entered into this file. In addition to the client's file, two loose-leaf binders are updated daily or as new information is obtained and furnished to the client's attorney. As it is compiled a review of the information with the client's attorney may be scheduled. This serves as documentation as the investigation progresses and as a means for honing leads represented by old and new information. The client's attorney, if they so request, may expect updates via the telephone and/or reports during the course of the investigation.

PI's see daily what clients are exposed to, hopefully, only once in their lifetime. I, personally, am inclined to be ultra sensitive to a client's feelings and emotions in order to shelter, as much as possible, having the client feel the deep sense of abandonment that often comes with the information we find. Human nature wants to deny betrayal by a loved one. I see this denial in almost every consultation where a loved one is suspected of infidelity. It would be great to find no incriminating information involving the subject of an investigation, for the sake of the client's self-esteem, confidence and well-being. However, more often than not, the opposite is true. The revelations of an investigation require carefully and thoughtfully chosen words when delivering the bad news. I recommend this not be done over the telephone or simply included with an invoice. I always meet with my clients in a supportive atmosphere; bearing in mind, this is most likely a once in a lifetime experience for the client.

TOOLS USED IN GATHERING INFORMATION

The crisp, clear February night in Indianapolis went unnoticed by the investigator, behind the darkened windows of the black Lincoln Towncar. Eyes, ears and mind were focused on an apartment on the other side of Arlington Place Apartments where the subject lives. "He's going to make a mistake, and when he does, I'll be there." The investigator believed this, however, after three days cooped up in a vehicle waiting for a clue, the investigator's confidence began to cloud with doubt. Suddenly, the light of the midnight moon lit up a male figure nervously walking across the parking lot. He carried a small, white, bathroom-sized garbage bag. Quickly, he tossed the bag into a huge open-mouthed dumpster, then hurried back to his small apartment, throwing nervous glances over each

DUMP DAY
GABAGE!
DUMPSTER

shoulder. From the shadows appeared the investigator, who began quietly and methodically digging for the disposable mistake. Within seconds, the investigator held the small white bag in his hands, still warm from the nervous grasp of the subject being watched. It must be something good. Who throws away garbage in the middle of the night? This small white plastic bag housed a clue, maybe large, maybe small, but a mistake worth the wait. The investigator returned to the motel room to examine the contents. The mistake turned out to be hidden inside a small cereal box. On a small pink *'While You Were Out'* note was written a name and post office box number from a small Missouri town. This became the key piece of information leading to the recovery of an abducted child missing for over eleven months.

As the child and I left the Mexican border town where I had found him, the "cereal box clue" raced through my memory once again. Perseverance and the very smallest of clues became the key to solving a case that had spanned the globe.

When working on any case, some or all of the many tools in an investigator's bag are used. The above story contains three key ingredients of the PI trade – patience, surveillance and sorting through discarded items. The process of working and solving cases involves gathering the information and, more importantly, knowing what to look for and what to do with the information. Many tools are used including surveillance, database research, sorting and identifying discarded and abandoned items, networking and good common investigative sense. These tools are the threads running through the fabric of our business.

PROPRIETARY DATABASE RESEARCH

Most reputable investigators subscribe to many proprietary databases. A proprietary database is an informational database not accessible by the general public. As the word "proprietary" indicates, these databases are exclusive to the field of private investigation and other organizations that fall under this umbrella, such as attorneys and some branches of law enforcement. Our agency uses no less than twenty different databases daily, with access to additional databases as they are needed. In most divorce cases, there is much more involved in an investigation than conducting surveillance, which is what most people associate with a private investigator. To obtain a very thorough and complete profile, it is important to engage in a very comprehensive investigation. Proprietary database research is an integral part of the process. The information provided by the client during the initial consultation should include as much known identifying information as possible. This information provides a solid basis in which to begin searching, documenting and compiling information. Database research, confirming and tracing residential history, criminal records, civil records and driving records may produce important information, leading to other unknown areas. Our agency subscribes to major nationwide proprietary databases, which provide criteria such as address, social security number, date of birth, employment history, and in some instances, relatives and neighbors.

The president of a local financial institution requested our services, stating he suspected his wife might be having an extramarital affair. The number one indicator of this was a non-existent sex life. His number one suspect was the tennis pro, with whom she had recently begun taking tennis lessons. After our initial consultation, we accepted his case. Using the information the client furnished and believed to be true, I followed the wife to the tennis courts where I observed her very friendly behavior with the tennis pro, but did not discover anything more. Soon, the animosity at home drove my client to move out of the family home and into his own duplex.

Around 6 p.m., while conducting surveillance at the wife's residence, several couples arrived, loaded camping gear into their vehicles and went to the lake for the weekend. After the weekend at the lake, a Jeep Wrangler was observed frequenting her house.

The Jeep was always backed into the garage making it impossible to get a tag number. A few days later a brand new Pontiac Trans Am began appearing in the driveway, along with the spouse's Suburban. The Trans Am was not yet tagged. We assumed it belonged to the wife, because it was constantly at her house; however, our client stated he was not aware of his wife purchasing a new vehicle. After a week or so, the Trans Am displayed a new tag, and we observed a man driving the car at different times. The tag was traced back to an unknown man, but the lien was in our client's wife's name.

Soon after this discovery, the children began telling our client stories about an *"Uncle Jerry,"* mom's friend, being a lot of fun. Further investigation revealed "Uncle Jerry" may have been fun, but had no United States driver's license and a revoked Canadian driver's license. We determined "Uncle Jerry" was actually from Canada, where he had a wife and children. Canadian authorities had filed attempted murder charges against "Uncle Jerry", claiming he forced the wife's vehicle (with his wife and one daughter inside) off the road, in an attempt to kill them. Attempted murder, assault and battery, as well as numerous domestic abuse complaints and charges were found against him. It was soon determined our client's wife was apparently supporting this man, who recently moved from a dumpy apartment on the east side of town into her upscale home. Based on this information, made possible through our surveillance efforts and the proprietary database information, our client's competent attorney was able to go to court, and obtain an emergency custody modification immediately awarding our client sole custody of his two children.

"Uncle Jerry's" true colors surfaced when he angrily followed the investigator out of the courtroom accusing him of lying about him on the witness stand. The judge ordered security to escort "Uncle Jerry" out of the courthouse, never to come back. Security then escorted the investigator to his vehicle without further incident.

SURVEILLANCE

As our office staff performs the database research, the investigator(s) will be in the field getting acquainted with the subject's neighborhood. Surveillance may begin immediately, to establish the routine of the subject and any identifiable patterns. Upfront knowledge of these patterns and routines will aid the investigator in setting up ongoing surveillance, which is another reason the client consultation is so important.

In most cases, surveillance is executed in the old fashioned way - putting in time observing the daily activities of a subject whether it is following them in a vehicle or on foot. Surveillance continues to be the most used tool in the majority of cases we see in our business. Current technology has made the art of surveillance more efficient for some investigations. The Global Positioning Satellite (GPS) tracking system, when attached to a subject's vehicle, may allow an investigator to essentially be in two places at one time.

It is very important to stress the in-depth screening process that should be administered before selling or leasing a GPS tracker to be installed on a vehicle. It is our agency's policy that a tracking device shall NOT be installed on a vehicle the client does not own or co-own. With that said, surveillance techniques have entered the twenty-first century, due to the GPS tracking system.

Should the client install a GPS tracker on a vehicle he or she owns, the technology allows an investigator to monitor the movements of the subject's vehicle with the GPS system. A computer monitor will reveal the location and status of the vehicle with the GPS tracker installed. If significant movement occurs, an investigator is able to immediately determine if a visual investigation is necessary. It may become clear that a closer look is needed *(as well as proof, as in photo and video)* based on the location of the subject's vehicle.

During a particular case, the husband suspected his wife might be having an affair but had no idea what she might be doing or with whom she might be doing it. Having just purchased his wife a new SUV, he leased a tracker and placed it on the vehicle. The wife was suspected of having an affair with a physician who worked with her at a local hospital. Our client requested our office monitor the GPS tracker he had installed on his vehicle, which was driven by his spouse. After three days of visual and video surveillance, we were successful in confirming that during after-work activities, the client's spouse was having an intimate, sexual relationship with the suspected physician. By monitoring the GPS tracker, we determined that when the two individuals left their evening shift at the hospital, they would each take different routes out of the parking area and rendezvous at what had previously been an unknown location. With the benefit of the tracking device, we were soon able to pinpoint these locations, wherein we observed a prominent physician, who was also married and the father of six children, having a torrid affair with our client's wife of ten plus years. One of their frequented locations was the secluded office of another physician, where they were able to park their cars in an area behind the office, out of sight from the main roadway, and enter through a back door, for their secret rendezvous. On other occasions, we located them in various back alleys and at a mini-storage property, where they would meet and use the physician's van to engage in their extramarital affair.

People tend to associate the work of a private investigator with the surveillance process, conjuring up images of trench coats and fedora hats, adorning the detective who stays several steps behind the subject, pausing in darkened doorways and behind lampposts, to avoid discovery. While trailing a subject on foot or by vehicle, the modern detective relies on various tools to assimilate information.

Each case is different; therefore, the degree to which each method is enlisted varies. In some cases, surveillance is the most important area of the investigation. Other cases may require very little time be spent scrutinizing a subject's whereabouts and more energy invested in database research, asset searches or other areas. Regardless of the tools used, the end result is a compilation of all information gathered during the course of the investigation. Once all of these pieces come together, the truth will begin to unfold.

DISCARDED AND ABANDONED ITEMS *(GARBAGE/ TRASH)*

Another valuable tool is sorting through discarded and abandoned items left curbside by the subject or paramour, commonly known as "trash." You have heard the old cliché: *"One man's trash is another man's treasure."* In the private investigation business, that statement could not be more true.

Many times we find insight into the life and actions of a subject through trash that proves to be invaluable. Information obtained by your investigator should provide specific and straightforward information; other information is but an ambiguous clue. When sorting, copying and itemizing discarded items, the obvious, as well as the vague clues are filed in a binder. Many times this will lead to something of extreme significance and will be the piece needed to solve a puzzling aspect of an investigation. You will note in many of the cases discussed, they have been won due to information retrieved from the subject's trash. This is a very powerful tool. Once trash is disposed of in a dumpster or at a curbside receptacle, any expectation of privacy is also discarded. Items left abandoned are fair game to anyone.

A couple, both alcoholics, filed for divorce. The judge declared the child be awarded to the mother ruling he felt she was the lesser of the two evils since she had gone through rehabilitation and had been sober for three months prior to the divorce. The father, who had not gone through rehabilitation, received standard visitation. Six months after the divorce, the father claimed to have completely stopped drinking and completed his rehabilitation. However, in the best interest of her daughter, the mother had obtained information that led her to suspect her ex-husband was still drinking, although she could not prove it. Approximately two years after the divorce, the mother moved to California with the child. When summer visitation came around, the father flew to California, picked up the child and brought her back to Oklahoma. After being in Oklahoma for a couple of weeks, the father filed a motion to modify custody. He claimed the mother was drinking again. Of course, he asserted he was sober and refused to return the child to California.

The mother contacted our office prior to the hearing to modify custody. She requested our assistance in proving or disproving her former husband was lying about his sobriety. Over a ninety-day period, leading up to a deposition for the modification hearing, we gathered the abandoned and discarded items from the ex-husband's residence. Every week numerous liquor bottles were recovered, indicating the subject was not just drinking, but drinking excessively. It also became evident, that because of her father's drinking, the child was spending most of her time with the paternal grandparents. However, during his deposition, the father profusely denied, under oath, drinking or even keeping alcohol in his home.

After the hearing began, five *cases* of empty liquor bottles were taken into the outer office of the judge's chambers. The father was put on the stand and questioned about his lifestyle, wherein he vehemently denied he was drinking. The investigator, being the only witness for the mother, was called to the witness stand following the father's testimony. As he passed the witness table, where the father sat, the smell of alcohol hung in the air. It must have been obvious to the judge, as well. The investigator completed his testimony, as to the liquor bottles found in the trash, and the defense rested. The court made its ruling, stating the case had been a huge waste of the court's time and ordered the child be returned to her mother instantly.

The number of times abandoned and discarded items have become an integral part of the persuading information is more than can be counted. Little thought is given to tossing trash bags into a dumpster or rolling the canister out to the curb. A mundane household duty performed on a daily or weekly basis by many of us, can play a major role in a legal battle. Knowing this, it is doubtful anyone reading this will ever look at trash in the same way again.

NETWORKING

It is important in solving certain cases to use confidential sources, informants and contacts. Sources and contacts are the name of the game in this business. The more people your investigator knows, in a variety of professions and locations, the better the investigation will be.

A seasoned investigator, with longevity in the private investigating field, will have developed numerous contacts such as bankers, mortgage brokers, insurance agents, investment brokers, medical professionals, law enforcement agents, and travel agents in addition to other private investigators throughout the United States and overseas. All are necessary and valuable in solving the puzzles investigators encounter.

However, the bulk of an investigation is done alone. Long, lonely hours spent deep in surveillance are where a PI may commonly be found. In that regard, a private investigator in today's world can be compared to the characters in a Mickey Spillane or Dashel Hammet novel. They are driven to do the work they do; it is in their blood. Most investigators are absorbed by their work and consider it their passion rather than just a job. The type of person often referred to as a workaholic appropriately describes a good PI.

All of my cases are punctuated with just a few moments, but one particular case comes to mind from several months ago, where being in the right place at the right exact moment provided the necessary foothold in the early stages of surveillance.

A prominent member of our community, I'll call her Jane, contacted our agency one winter afternoon with a bit of a heavy heart and a nagging suspicion. I met her at a local hotel restaurant and observed an attractive middle-aged woman wearing a confidence defined by her successful career, yet in her eyes I saw a quiet insecurity, perhaps because she believed the love of her life was having a romantic affair with another woman. After greeting formalities, she quickly and nervously began to unfold the short story that caused her to seek our agency's help. Although she could articulate her suspicion, she was clearly in denial, as she kept reassuring herself that it was probably nothing. "I don't think anything is going on, but I need to find out," she began, with those famous opening words of one being betrayed.

She had noticed subtle differences over the past six to eight months *(typical signs of a cheating heart)* but did not become concerned until she walked in on an unusual situation. Her husband's office was located within walking distance from their home. Periodically, Jane would walk over to Richard's office just to say hello and offer assistance, if needed. This particular evening, around six o'clock, Jane entered the office as normal, but encountered a scene that seemed suspicious to her. Her husband casually sat in his office, entertaining with conversation and a scotch, a beautiful young girl in a rather short skirt. She appeared to be not much older than his oldest child. The girl sat bare-footed with her legs tucked under her. She seemed very comfortable with her surroundings. Richard greeted Jane and calmly explained he was busy with a client. Jane apologized for the intrusion, excused herself and walked back home fighting with her intuition.

Later that evening at home, Jane confronted her husband about what she had observed and asked if there was anything to it. Richard assured her nothing was going on and explained that the woman was a new client, who had entered his office upset and had requested a drink. He said he poured himself a drink out of politeness and began the consultation with the client, which is when Jane walked in. Jane wanted to believe his story. In fact, this mantra of belief freely flowed from her mouth frequently. Yet, she is here speaking with me, a private investigator, so obviously her heart does not believe him. Let this be a reminder that your intuition is usually accurate.

Without gathering anymore information, I advised the client that if she wanted to find out the truth without further adieu, she should go visit her family over the upcoming weekend, putting her suspicions out of her mind and let me see what I could find out. She agreed and made the necessary arrangements to leave town with the kids on Friday, leaving her husband behind. I established surveillance, prior to Jane's departure, and observed the "happy family" lovingly saying good-byes. The *"doting father"* stood smiling and waving in the yard, watching his family fade into the distance. He stood there, casually dressed, for a good five minutes until they were completely out of sight. I watched him jog into the house and a short time later emerge a new man, walking like a version of his youth, wearing a dapper sports coat. I could just imagine the tune he might be humming, *"Are You Lonesome Tonight?"* as he effortlessly slid into his gold Mercedes. I followed him to the neighborhood liquor store where he purchased four bottles of wine, then to the nearest convenience store where he bought cigarettes. Once he had the necessary items, he bolted onto the highway and headed west at a high rate of speed, obviously eager and excited about his journey. I followed him to a suburb of the city and into an upper middle class neighborhood. He began driving around the neighborhood, as if he was making sure he was not being followed.

I stopped my car and raised the hood as if having car trouble, so as not to blow my cover. Unsure of his destination, I kept an eye out for him. I was in the right place at the right time. I witnessed firsthand the opening of a garage door, the subject quickly whipping his vehicle into the garage and the door immediately closing, taking no more than twenty seconds. This type of discovery causes a private investigator to want to dance in the streets! But I was too busy video documenting the activities of the subject.

At the client's request, the case continued for six months, in order to establish concrete documentation of a long-term affair rather than an incident, which could be explained as a one-time mistake. Once the client was satisfied with the information, she confronted her spouse and, after much deliberation, an eventual reconciliation occurred, with the couple vowing to be more honest.

As you can see, reasons for hiring an investigator are as unique as the person doing the hiring. Of course, human nature always carries the possibility of surprise, but my experience suggests that people are, for the most part, very predictable.

Welcome to my world. On the one hand there are the subjects who live in an atmosphere of deceit, betrayal and avoidance of the truth. On the other hand are my clients. Those who have been lied to and betrayed and are usually in a lot of pain. My job is to find the truth and it lies somewhere in between.

Two

Top Ten Reasons to Hire a PI

It was in an upscale hotel lobby where I was introduced to a lovely and quite stylish woman. I began the conversation by telling her I was a private investigator and the woman followed by telling me her birth mother had left her when she was four years old. I was enormously impressed by the woman, eager to get to know her better, but searching for her birth mother also intrigued me.

Seldom do I take off my PI hat. Over the next couple of weeks by researching a simple paper trail, I came up with several potential leads, giving me reason to contact the woman again. My intuition seemed to tell me this was an extraordinary woman but little did I know this would lead to a life-long relationship.

Our phone may ring tomorrow describing a story I have never heard before, but true to the "seen-it-all-before" character type of pulp fiction; however, I doubt it. Most cases fall into one of a few categories. Some investigators specialize in a particular area but most first-rate investigators are capable of handling the surprising aspects of this business.

Regardless of the state of the nation or the economy, business for most responsible private investigators stays relatively steady. Our agency, located in an Oklahoma City suburb, tries to maintain a very balanced caseload. If necessary I will decline a case, if I believe our staff is working at our most efficient capacity. We try to keep our office staff's workload at a level where they can stay caught up on their duties and the investigators are able to work "*normal*" hours.

Many businesses experience a slump after the holidays. The cash is not flowing after over-extending one's credit cards and checkbook. The holiday season occasionally prompts an unspoken "break in fighting" among domestic affairs and the associated arguing. However, within a few days the players revert to their old tricks. Immediately following the holiday season, it is not unusual for the number of potential clients, calling our office to exceed twenty to twenty-five calls a day. Our office is usually a whirlwind of activity. We have a motto adopted from a film, "As long as people lie, cheat, and steal, we'll always have a job." This has proven to be true over the course of the past quarter of a century, no matter the economic climate.

Men and women alike retain our services for many different reasons. Based on our experience, we have developed a top ten list of reasons why a person might hire a private investigator. There are as many reasons as there are people, a million variations on a theme. This list is merely the top ten reasons compiled by our office.

Top Ten Reasons to Hire a PI

10. Insurance and Workers' Compensation Fraud
9. Locating and Uncovering Hidden Assets
8. Boyfriend, Lover, or Prospective Partner's History
7. Parental GPS Tracking of New Teenager Drivers
6. Criminal Investigations
5. Covert Video Monitoring of Elder Abuse
4. Stalking Victims and/or Witness Harassment
3. Locating Biological Parents, Children or Siblings
2. Child Custody and Modification of Custody

And the Number One reason for hiring a PI is...

1. Suspicion of a Cheating Spouse

Not all cases accepted by a private investigator are lengthy and in-depth. While some cases may take years to solve, others may close in less than a week. Some cases, such as a background search or locating a birth parent, may seem small compared to those of divorce and custody cases, but to the client, the goals are just as important. The above Top Ten List will be discussed in this chapter with the exception of the top two reasons, which have earned a chapter of their own.

10. Insurance and Workers' Compensation Fraud

Some investigators concentrate on working for insurance companies or private corporations, investigating only workers' compensation claims. Employees injured at work during the course of their duties are the most common of this type of investigation. The employee may be entitled to compensation for work missed while recovering from the on-the-job injury. Two main questions asked, in order to establish liability of the employer are: *"Was the person in fact an employee at the time of injury?"* and *"Did the injury occur during the scope of employment (was the injury a result of required job duties)?"*

If a fraudulent claim has been filed, the best-case scenario for the insurance company is to find proof the claimant is working at another job while collecting compensation for an injury. Another scenario is to obtain documentation of the claimant engaged in activities contradictive to his post-injury condition.

A recent case, involving a worker's compensation claim, began when an employee of a daycare, filed against her employer, claiming she had injured her back while dusting, with a feather duster, no less. Our client believed this claim was bogus and needed proof. Following this subject was not very exciting, but very productive. Still photographs and video were obtained of the subject carrying large garbage bags of trash and heaving them into the dumpster, as well as lifting and carrying her young child on her hip. We captured lasting impressions of her bending forward at the waist to pick things up, lifting heavy objects and throwing objects (trash) over her shoulder. To put the icing on the cake, we watched her, through our camera lenses, falling for the oldest trick in the book – stooping to pick up several quarters, dimes and nickels lying on the pavement beside her car. When performing surveillance in this type of case, it is very important extreme tactics are not used. By this, I mean tactics more extreme than the one described above, dropping a few coins in order to obtain verification the subject is not incapacitated as he or she claims. Through covert surveillance, an investigator may obtain all the necessary information without resorting to contrived methods. The coin method may be used to expedite the duration of the case and to show the range of motion of which the subject is capable. Applying extreme methods in order to prove a false claim is not only unethical, but it can sabotage the case for the client.

For example, if some sort of heavy object is planted in the path of a subject and entices the subject to pick it up or move it, in some way that could possibly contradict the medical claim. However, there are a couple of things that could jeopardize the litigation. If the subject was truly injured on the job and the rehabilitation process was nearing a successful completion, negative tactics could cause re-injury, prolonging the compensation time period. In the same vein, if the subject was faking an injury, instead of proving this, it is very possible he or she could actually become injured, due to the use of unethical methods, which could be considered entrapment and might not be allowed in court. The client could also be sued if this were to happen.

9. Locating and Uncovering Hidden Assets

Uncovering hidden assets may also fall under the heading of divorce. This service is generally not requested alone. It is somewhat common to discover one party or the other hiding marital assets in order to avoid sharing those assets at the time of divorce. Anyone contemplating divorce or who finds themselves the victim of divorce should request this type of investigation. In many cases, one spouse or the other has been kept out of the financial loop and has no idea about their joint business affairs.

Uncovering hidden assets can be as simple as matching the subject's tax returns to his income. However, in most cases, some digging is required. The PI will often covertly investigate the business of friends or associates, of the subject, to find a trail that will lead to the hiding place.

Debbie's story is a perfect example. She had been married for almost thirty years and described her role in the marriage as being subservient, reminiscent of the fifties housewife. She ran the household and raised the children, while her husband's career flourished. The picture painted for the world was of a happy family, but what the world did not see was the emotional and physical abuse that went on behind closed doors.

As with many marriages, extramarital relations are not surprising, except to the wife or husband who is being cheated on. Debbie was no exception. Although her marriage was far from perfect and her husband was abusive, she was still shocked when she discovered he was cheating. The shock doubled when her discovery led to her husband filing for divorce. The divorce process turned ugly, as happens many times, especially when infidelity is involved. Pain and frustration lead to power struggles. In Debbie's case, her entire lifestyle was being turned upside down and the only job she had been doing, for the past fifteen years -- raising children -- was being threatened.

As with many women who play the traditional wifely role, knowledge of the family financial situation may be practically non-existent. Therefore, Debbie's spouse hid assets throughout their marriage. Had she not hired an investigator, her settlement would have been meager at best, certainly not a reflection of years of devotion to her husband and family.

In our initial consultation, the client revealed she did not even know where her spouse was living. He had moved out of the marital residence, leaving Debbie with two minor children, very little money and absolutely no communication. Further, Debbie kept insisting money was tight because her spouse was telling her the past couple of years had been difficult financially and they simply had no extra money. Debbie accepted her spouse's statements, believing the man she had devoted her life to would never lie to her. The fact that he was "having an affair" was inconceivable. I asked Debbie why she was so sure her spouse was not romantically involved with anyone, to which she replied, *"I asked him and he said, 'Absolutely not, you know I love you.'"* Debbie had learned to accept and believe her spouse was married to his work, usually leaving his office no earlier than 6:30 p.m. and as late as 8:30 p.m.

Had Debbie's parents not insisted she find out the truth, Debbie could have easily kept her head buried in the sand and never have known the extent of her spouse's activities, which included hiding assets reaching the high six figures. After accepting this case, the wayward spouse's address was determined to be in an upper-class town home with a "rear-entry" double garage, in a very prestigious area of Oklahoma City. Our client had advised us she believed her spouse to be not only drinking heavily, but a complete alcoholic.

On the third evening of the investigation, at 5:45 p.m., surveillance was established in the parking lot of the spouse's high-rise office building. Being wintertime, it was dark by 6 p.m. Lights were on in the offices and from our surveillance location; we had a clear view into the subject's third floor offices.

Within a short time of surveillance being established, we noticed everyone appeared to have left the office building except for our subject and one attractive blond, who appeared to be several years younger than our subject. With the night-vision camera rolling, we were able to confirm, without a doubt, our client's spouse was having an affair. After pouring several drinks, the two began removing their clothes, the rest of their meeting was on film and revealed their actions were less than business like. As the investigation continued, we determined the "attractive blond" was actually a former assistant to our client's spouse.

Digging deeper into the subject's activities, we were able to confirm that a sizable portion of his earnings were being deposited into a corporate bank account, with the *"President"* being none other than the paramour. The same paramour we had observed and photographed *"taking care of business"* in his office. It was also learned the paramour's luxury automobile had no lien. A subpoena of the dealer's *'Bill of Sale'* revealed that our subject had indeed paid cash for the young woman's vehicle.

Apparently, this affair had been going on since his *"assistant"* quit working in the office four years earlier. During these four years, she had obtained a divorce from her spouse and moved into a lovely condominium, within walking distance of her wealthy lover. When the attorney began 'discovery,' the subject furnished financial documents quite different from certain financial documents we were able to acquire, throughout this investigation.

Under oath, the subject was questioned about the validity of the documents he had furnished, swearing they were all true and correct. These documents reflected ALL of his income, ALL of his savings, etc. Following this testimony, our client's attorney asked the subject to explain certain documents we had retrieved through our investigation. When confronted with the true information, the subject began to retract his statements, and it was ultimately determined he had been keeping TWO complete, yet distinctly different, sets of financial records, as well as depositing thousands and thousands of dollars into the paramour's account.

When all was totaled and the divorce was granted, the Court was able to determine our client's share of the marital estate was some $800,000 more than she would have received, had she chosen to believe her spouse, rather than obtain the services of a private investigator. Our client was grateful her parents had the wisdom to encourage her to pursue the truth.

Debbie's story exemplifies the type of case in which a client is ideally served by a private investigator's expertise in a financial probe. The discovery of hidden assets was indispensable to her welfare. Hiring a private investigator insured her of a successful outcome.

8. Boyfriend, Lover or Prospective Partner's History

Abby called our office, after returning from a trip to North Carolina. On the return flight home, she sat next to a gentleman, with whom a passionate conversation transpired. By the end of the two and a half hour flight, she was smitten and the feeling seemed to be returned by him. Based on their lengthy conversation, they appeared to be of the same social and economic stature, as well as, having similar interests and beliefs. Several days after landing on Oklahoma soil, Abby was still flying high. A date had been discussed for the following week, but due to her age and experience, she knew better than to blindly enter into a relationship. That is where I came in.

Abby was blessed with the luxury and sometimes burden of wealth and prominent social standing. In previous romantic relationships, she had been burned several times, by men interested only in her financial "bottom line." Being cautious may dim the spontaneity somewhat, but it was a measure she didn't feel she could afford to by-pass this time. She had never hired an investigator, especially not in these matters. Abby began her initial conversation with me, like most of my other clients, nervous and embarrassed. A complete background check was prescribed, since Abby's main concern was whether or not the man was who and what he claimed to be. The bulk of the investigation was performed at my computer, using various proprietary databases, a few phone calls and only two trips to the courthouse, to get original copies of a civil file.

After a few days of investigating and much to Abby's relief, we were able to determine she had snagged quite a catch. Now the rest was up to Abby.

7. Parental GPS Tracking of New Teenage Drivers

We are thankful for the advanced technology we have access to in this century. The ability to know the whereabouts and safety of our children and elderly family members is much easier and it has become a highly requested service. Video surveillance cameras and GPS tracking systems are used regularly, especially in cases related to the welfare of those for whom we are most responsible.

Everyone has heard of the "Nanny Cam" and the media attention surrounding it. Through the services of a private investigator, daily activities of a caregiver or babysitter can be covertly monitored, as well as physical surveillance and appropriate background research.

The GPS tracking system is also perfect for installation in your teenager's vehicle. In today's world, there is not enough that can be done to protect our children. In most cases, it is not that parents do not trust their child or want to keep tabs on his or her every move. It is the contrary; it is those people in the world looking to harm innocent children, whom parents do not and should not trust. Fortunately, tracking teenagers has provided us with many interesting stories to tell and has assisted in helping situations, that otherwise may have come to a tragic ending. In fact, it has proven to be a real eye-opener for many parents. This great tool for caring parents gives them a sense of security when they know their teenager will occasionally leave out crucial information. While I feel a great sense of reward from this job and with all the various cases I work, helping a parent find peace of mind, concerning the safety of their teen, is most gratifying. The daily monitoring has turned up certain episodes, which have become important issues pertaining to teenage driving and their whereabouts, and have assisted parents in knowing how to deal with their teenager.

Sam had just completed his driver's education course and passed his driving test. He had been driving with a permit under parent supervision and had proven himself to be a conscientious driver. Once he was awarded his driver's license, his parents delivered a well maintained, although slightly used, metallic blue Ford Mustang equipped with a covertly installed GPS tracking devise. Sam was unaware of the added feature, but totally aware of the power of his new Mustang. He continued to be a safe and dependable driver, only going to and from school or other acceptable destinations. Then one afternoon, he traveled a couple of miles north of his usual route and almost doubled his highest rate of speed. This slight detour could have cost Sam his life or, at a minimum, his license. When his parents saw this report, they both realized what he was doing – letting the Mustang run wide open on a secluded road. This behavior was not a major concern until it became a more frequent habit and he began speeding within the city limits. Sam's parents monitored this newfound freedom over the course of a couple of months. Soon Sam's driving reverted back to the predictable routine he had established upon receiving the privilege and responsibility of his first car. I did not ask his parents how they addressed this situation but it was successful.

Considering that motor vehicle crashes are the leading cause of death for 15 to 20 year olds in the United States and almost half of the 5,341 deaths among this age group, reported in 2001, were due to speeding,4 every effort made to protect our teens is well advised.

Several programs are already in existence, to aid in watching out for teenagers. Some of these programs utilize a bumper sticker and depend on concerned citizens to report observed speeding or erratic behavior. These work similar to the bumper stickers you see on trucks and school buses. An 800 number is provided on the bumper sticker, along with an identifying number encouraging the concerned driver to call. This is a wonderful attempt to help keep our young people alive. Short of a program such as Graduated Driver Licensing, which has been proven successful in Canada and New Zealand, or imposing restrictions as Maryland and California have done, which have resulted in lowering fatal crash statistics,5 it is up to parents to take the matter of keeping their children alive and safe into their own hands.

The best tool, our office has seen, is the use of a GPS tracking system. Rather than relying on a concerned citizen, to take the time to call an 800 number, when they witness irresponsible driving, the parents have a daily real-time way of keeping an eye on their teen. This allows the parents to be pro-active, regarding the safety of their child and assume a sense of security in a potentially reckless situation.

6. Criminal Investigations

The typical criminal case we handle falls under a background search. A client may need criminal history on an employee, potential spouse, or family member. The majority of the work is researched in our office using proprietary databases, as well as the appropriate courthouse(s).

We do not normally investigate actual criminal cases, although, we have become involved in several cases of this nature, over the course of our career. Generally, when our services are engaged, it is prior to any criminal charges being filed. For example, several years ago a man named John, who suspected his wife was having an affair, hired us. As you know, this is the most common case seen in our office. The case seemed very run of the mill. Information was gathered and presented to our client, substantiating his suspicions.

As with many cases of this nature, the client was not ready to accept the truth. He went through the typical period of denial. It is typically during this period that a client might request further proof, for no other reason than to have time to adjust to the reality of what we have learned. When John called for an additional consultation, soon after learning of his wife's affair, I expected him to ask to continue the investigation, in order to gain additional confirmation. I was very surprised when he nervously requested a bodyguard, because he feared his life was in danger. This unexpected twist took what seemed to be a very typical case into a new direction. Unfortunately, it quickly and certainly became criminal before his request for a bodyguard could be fulfilled. When my client went to pick up his children for visitation he was murdered in the garage of his home. Apparently his wife and her lover had been plotting to begin a new life together, leaving the details to the devil, which included living off my client's life insurance policy. They began a new life, although not together, for they are both now living on death row.

The following story is much more representative of the type of work we generally do, involving criminal investigations. We were hired, by a defense attorney, to gather information on the party of the opposing side. The case involved child molestation charges, against the stepfather of a young girl, initiated by the girl's biological father. We were hired to investigate if the biological father's motives stemmed from retaliation, against the biological mother. She had recently filed a motion to modify custody against the former spouse, and had been awarded increased child support and his visitation was decreased.

This investigation involved background interviews and research of all parties associated with the biological father and his wife. Our instructions were to find any information that might discredit the claims or the character of the claimant. In this case, through our normal means, we were able to find enough debatable information, to cause the biological father's intentions to be questioned.

As you can see, a criminal investigation can branch off into many different areas. While we may not be on the front end of a murder investigation or other type of felony investigations, our involvement stems from other aspects, which can feed into a criminal investigation, as described in the above cases. Behind the scenes is where we prefer to be involved when investigating criminal cases.

5. Video Monitoring of Elder Abuse

The concern for the safety of a senior citizen is as equally important for family members, as monitoring the safety of teenage drivers. For peace of mind, a covert video surveillance camera can be installed in an elderly parent's home or assisted-living residence in order to monitor the activities of the caregiver. If need be, under-cover work can be performed in nursing home situations, to get additional knowledge, as to what is going on with the care of a loved one, who is dependent upon the facility.

Also, there comes a time when the elderly can no longer safely operate a vehicle. It is hard for a family member to bring up the subject without offending their loved one. The best answer might be as simple as installing a Global Positioning Satellite tracking device in the senior citizen's vehicle. This allows the senior adult to maintain their driving independence, while those concerned maintain their peace of mind. When performed in this manner, their safety and ability can be monitored, without stripping them of their dignity.

One of our first tracking devices, purchased by one of our clients, was installed on the vehicle of the client's elderly father. The family grew more and more concerned with his safety while he was out and about town, due to recent bouts of losing his way back home. On a few occasions, he had driven himself to an appointment or destination, and upon time to return home, he became confused as to how to get there. Each time he called his son and asked for help, which led the family to my office. It was very important to them that their elder's independent spirit remain intact, but they needed peace of mind. Monitoring this system is as easy as pointing and clicking a mouse. We are able to generate reports for specific days and times, as well as, view a real-time map indicating the activities of the vehicle. This allows us to apply virtual vehicle surveillance, without leaving our office. Since this technology is at our fingertips, we sometimes take a few moments periodically throughout the day to analyze the activity. This procedure paid off for the above client. You, as the client should have power of attorney or other legal authority before installing a GPS tracker.

One morning, while doing our periodic analysis of the patriarch's vehicle, we noticed it was stopped an extraordinary amount of time in what appeared to be an intersection. We called our client and gave him the location of his father's vehicle, advising him it might be beneficial to check in on him. Sure enough, our client found his father had been involved in a minor accident; fortunately, he was not injured; only bewildered.

This is a good time to reiterate the serious nature involved when using standard investigative tools. The GPS tracker is no different than any other tool used in the business of private investigation, if it is used conscientiously after pre-investigation screening. A reputable investigator will not take a case without knowing who their client is, their motive for hiring an investigator and what they intend to do with the information gathered. As stated in Chapter One, in our offices we never install a tracking device, on a vehicle, our client does not own, co-own or have other legal authority to do so. In cases monitoring an elder, the client is the child or spouse of the subject we are hired to investigate or monitor for safety reasons. In the case of teenage driver safety, the client is the parent or legal guardian. It would not be prudent to track the whereabouts of a person, for reasons that may not be legal or other than those already mentioned.

4. Stalking Victims and/or Witness Harassment

Several years ago, a young woman, who felt an unknown man was stalking her, contacted our office. She related the occasions she had mentally filed away as just coincidence. Some instances she never actually saw anyone, but her intuition warned her of potential danger. There were other specific instances, where she recalled actually seeing this man, who had a non-descript and unassuming manner. He seemed intent upon her presence, and each time the hair on the back of her neck stood up. This was the same reaction her body had, even when the man was not visible to her. After a few weeks of these encounters, she finally decided to trust her intuition and hire someone to get to the bottom of this.

Action was taken immediately, by setting up surveillance cameras, focused on her front and back porches and her bedroom window. She had not related any concern or incident regarding these areas, but to be safe, all bases were covered. At her request, we also began following her throughout her daily activities. The results were quick and alarming.

By the end of the first week, we observed and consequently video recorded, this woman being stalked five out of six days. And six out of six days, video information was collected of a man standing in the shadows near each entrance of her home; pacing back and forth between the front door and the back door, stopping at times near her bedroom window. During the first day of surveillance, the subject was followed back to his place of employment and then later that evening, back to his place of residence. With this information, the subject's identity was soon determined.

Before showing her the information collected, confirming the danger of which her intuition warned her, we asked her if she had been aware of her stalker over the past week. She said she had the same feeling of fear, which manifested itself at the nape of her neck everyday, but she only actually saw the man a couple of times. She was not prepared for what she saw on the video. The realization of what she viewed left her visibly shaken. Fortunately, the identity and background research reassured her that her stalker did not have a criminal history. This man was not someone she knew, and, as it turned out, he was a somewhat mentally challenged young man with a romantic obsession for her, claiming he "watched over her" for her protection.

In this situation, trusting her intuition and seeking help was the right thing for our client to do. In fact, you will not go wrong, if you follow those simple steps in any situation. When dealing with a stalker, you may want to answer questions such as:

- ✓ Do you recognize the person stalking you?
- ✓ Could this person be a former spouse or jilted lover?
- ✓ Do you recall even a casual acquaintance or colleague from work?
- ✓ Is this person a complete stranger?
- ✓ Have you talked to, had a drink with or danced with this person at a bar?

While attempting to determine the client's connection or link to the stalker, we also assess the potential for bodily harm. If we believe there is a real potential for danger, it may be recommended the victim file for a "victim's protective order" followed by law enforcement being notified and by their assistance being requested. On another occasion, we were retained to investigate, what was believed to be a stalker situation. The case actually turned out to be a serious case of "witness harassment."

Our client, a female, who was served with a subpoena to appear as a witness for the plaintiff (wife) in a bitter divorce and child custody case, became the harassed victim. The defendant (husband), with the help of a "buddy" attempted to dissuade the witness from testifying against the plaintiff's husband.

It is becoming more common for a witness, plaintiff or defendant to be placed under surveillance, by the opposing side, to determine credibility, or lack thereof, and attempt to use any adverse information to their advantage.

In many of these cases, a professional private investigator will be retained to conduct the investigation to avoid any suspicion of harassment or stalking. However, if the sole purpose of retaining an investigator is to intimidate a witness, you should bring this to the immediate attention of your attorney, as there may be grounds for legal action to curtail the investigation.

On the flip side, our services have been engaged to determine if the client or the client's witnesses are being harassed, and if so, to what extent.

3. Locating Biological Parents, Children and Siblings

Locating a person, be it a biological parent, child, sibling, or a long-lost friend, may be researched in a similar way, using our proprietary databases. This type of investigation may also require interviewing extended family members and neighbors.

Upon completing the in-take sheet with a potential client over the phone, an investigation firm with our experience will have a good idea how long it will take to find a subject and which sources to use. This is one of the purposes for gathering information during the initial contact for all cases – to ascertain the probability, as well as, our anticipated success by taking the case.

If the subject's name is common, the search will require more steps to narrow it down and determine the location of the correct person. The more databases researched and the more time spent equals a higher charge to the client. An unusual or less common name is usually easier to successfully locate and requires less time and effort.

We have had our share of odd cases over the years, but none quite as unusual as this one. This was our first and only assignment to find a missing horse. That's right, a horse. A six-year-old Paint gelding, blaze with four stockings, was abducted by the client's ex-boyfriend, who had reportedly taken the beloved steed (Dakota) out of state. Our job was to determine the location of Dakota. The owner of Dakota advised us his markings were very distinct and identifiable and furnished us with several photographs of the horse. In a field of Paints, our client would have quickly and assuredly picked out her baby. But for a man, who had not spent much time among the four-legged kind in more than twenty years, this presented quite a challenge. I once owned a ranch with several horses, but it still did not qualify me as a horse-authority or match the level of knowledge to distinguish similar horses apart, as my client was easily able to do. I drove through rural countrysides, spanning three states, trying to match the many Paint horses to the pictures of Dakota. Of all the pictures I gathered of various horses, none was identified as the missing and elusive Dakota, much to the dismay and sadness of my client.

Unfortunately, searching for a horse requires manpower and Dakota not being listed on any of the proprietary people databases we had to focus on the abductor. All of the typical investigative tools were used to locate the whereabouts of the abductor, which should have led us to the horse. Disappointingly, it never did. Had the client contacted us when the horse was first abducted it is very possible the tracks to Dakota would have still been warm. It was determined, that between the time Dakota was abducted and the time my agency was hired, the former boyfriend had already profited by selling the horse at one of the numerous horse sales across the state. Dakota could be on any rural road, in any town, in any state. I still find myself noticing every Paint gelding I see, while driving along country roads and wondering about the missing horse, Dakota.

Now let us go from following a horse trail back to the proverbial paper trail. I will continue with the story, which began this chapter. I spoke earlier of finding the right niche that led me directly to the mother of the beautiful young woman I had encountered in a hotel lobby. Personal interest in this woman, Carrie, prompted me to do some preliminary work regarding the search for her biological mother.

I had begun to put together initial pieces to the puzzle, but because her mother had given up custody over thirty years prior and was only 17 or 18 at the time, I needed more specific information. The trail of names I had tried to follow were vague up to this point, so I called to request any documentation she might have relating to her father, who had maintained parental rights.

After returning from military duty in Germany, he shuffled the responsibility of Carrie and her brother to his parents. Carrie's father was now deceased, but she eagerly assured me she would promptly contact her stepmother, with whom she had maintained a good relationship over the years. Within the week, I sat pouring over files from Carrie's father's estate, which included two conflicting birth certificates for Carrie and a document relinquishing parental rights, signed by her mother, Louise. Again, most of the names, like Williams, Smith and Johnson, were so common it was going to be extremely time consuming to begin to follow. However, on the document relinquishing parental rights, I found a more unusual name, Dimas. This name took me to the first solid step that would become a direct path to Carrie's mother. Doris Dimas had signed, as a witness, to Louise's signature. Through my database research, I discovered Mrs. Dimas lived in Tennessee; however, she had an unlisted number. So as not to offend her sensibility, I sent a telegram asking her to get in touch with me, regarding a very important matter. It was not long until this very elegant and colorful woman telephoned. When I explained who I was and who I was looking for, Doris assumed it pertained to Louise's abusive father. Doris was Louise's half-sister and in a protective nature, she offered to contact Louise who would in turn contact me, if appropriate. The dots were beginning to connect. Only a couple more pieces and the picture would be complete.

I did not have to wait long before receiving a phone call from Louise, who was now remarried and living in Alabama. After a brief introduction, I got right to the point and asked if she was the mother of

a girl named Carrie. With a gasp, she tearfully replied, "You're an answer to my prayers." Then a flood of questions about her daughter erupted. Due to confidentiality, I was not at liberty to elaborate more than some obscure details of Carrie. I did tell her she was a beautiful, educated and professional young woman. The conversation ended with Louise saying she would like to visit with her pastor before contacting her daughter. It was agreed that she would call me when she felt she was ready, for the reality of her answered prayers. A couple of days after the initial conversation with Louise, my telephone rang. The maternal voice on the other end nervously asked to schedule a telephone meeting with Carrie.

Have You Seen Me?
missing
Born
Name

The following Wednesday evening, at 6 p.m., was the agreed upon day and time.

It was a Wednesday evening when I placed the call to Louise. She had advised she would miss church to wait for the call. It was not so simple on this end. Carrie's dream of knowing her birth mother was literally at her fingertips, yet she was terrified by the prospect of picking up the phone. She lamented to her stepmother that she had no idea what to say to her mother or even how to address her. Her stepmother encouraged her to make the call and let nature take its course.

I agreed to meet Carrie at my office to provide moral support and to make the introductory call. Minutes before I picked up the phone to place the call, I assured Carrie she was under no obligation or pressure of any kind to speak to her mother. The plan was for me to keep up my end of the deal by placing the call, but when I handed the phone to her, she was free to hang up if she chose. With a very nervous woman by my side, I rang Louise's number. The call was answered on the first ring. Skipping the exchange of customary pleasantries, I informed Louise, "The next voice you hear will be your daughter's." I turned, offering the phone to Carrie, who with wide, startled eyes, grabbed the receiver and began the first emotional and heart-warming conversation with, "Hello, Mother?"

They both cried thirty years of tears, accented with smiles and laughter along the way. The ninety-minute conversation ended, but a family renaissance began. Louise sent airline tickets to Carrie and her brother Stan. I have had the pleasure of watching the relationship between Carrie and her mother grow over the years. As Carrie renewed her bond with her mother, Carrie and I formed a bond of our own, creating a paper trail endorsed by the court clerk of a small town in Texas, namely a marriage license.

Obviously, not all of my cases have a happy ending or the same level of involvement. I cannot, however, claim a detachment from my cases, because the shear nature of what I do involves the very lives of human beings. I am genuinely concerned about the well-being of my clients and feel dedicated to helping them in my own unique way. All of the technology in the world does not replace human interaction. I take this business quite seriously.

Now that you are familiar with the most common cases handled in our office, you can imagine how infinite the possibilities are as to why a person might require the services of a private investigator. There are as many reasons as there are people. However, the type of case we see most often in our business is related to divorce and the variations within this field are many.

Three

The Role of a PI in a Divorce Case

A trip to the Cayman Islands is common among the upper crust of society. Nothing would be thought out of the ordinary about frequenting this sunny oasis two or three times a year, unless you are in the process of divorcing a woman, who funded your business with her personal money and you are attempting to get half of everything that rightfully belongs to her. The fact that she suspects you of having a girlfriend and hiding money, makes those ordinary trips stand out like a sore thumb. This is where I made my entrance. After a few trips to the Cayman Islands, we had the information to prove both suspicions.

The preceding story was extracted from an actual case file and is an example of hidden asset discovery. Concerns about monetary issues are real when a marital relationship is ending. Sometimes having a good attorney, to help insure an equitable settlement, may not be enough. This is why divorce is another reason people hire private investigators. It is usually due to suspicions of infidelity, although that is not always the primary reason our services are solicited. Allocation of marital finances to a paramour and confirmation of a paramour are only pieces to the puzzle. Determining the lifestyle, stability of a parent, possible criminal activity, as well as discovering hidden assets all goes hand in hand with many divorce-related cases. If you find yourself at a crossroad and suspect that one road might be leading to divorce, you may be overwhelmed with unfamiliar emotions. If this is your first experience with divorce, knowing what to do next can be just as overwhelming.

The following information, provided by the Oklahoma Bar Association, may help you get started. Since each state is governed by their own set of laws, you should research the laws in your state, to determine how each aspect of the divorce process is handled. For example, in Oklahoma there are twelve grounds acceptable for divorce but only a few are commonly used, such as incompatibility, gross neglect of duty to support, extreme physical or mental cruelty, abandonment for a period of one year, and adultery.6 The state you reside in may, or may not, accept similar grounds.

In a no-fault divorce state, it may not be necessary to prove certain grounds for a divorce. Fifteen states offer only no-fault divorces, which may expedite the process and prioritize custody, child support, and other important issues. In certain other states, the residents are given the option of choosing either no-fault divorce or fault divorce. There are only seven states where no-fault divorces are not allowed, of these seven states, two (New York and North Carolina) are in the top five highest number of divorces, reported during the year of 2003.7

These figures fall slightly below the national average divorce rate of 3.8 per 1,000.8 Two opposite arguments exist for each approach. Some believe fault-divorce would reduce marital breakdown. Others argue that no-fault divorce protects the rights of individuals. The argument, claiming fault-divorce reduces the risk of divorce, is not supported based on the above-mentioned facts. Several states are in the process of implementing tougher divorce requirements in an effort to decrease the soaring rate of divorce.

Whereas both parties assume responsibility in no-fault divorce the process can be amicable, there are those individuals who choose to go to war and invest enormous amounts of time and money rather than compromise. This adversarial approach has become more common than not.

When one party or the other does not agree on key elements the divorce is contested, and when both parties agree on key elements the divorce is uncontested. While divorce may be approached in different ways, the basic procedure will be similar. Statutes however, may differ greatly from one state to another. For example, in Oklahoma, once a petition for divorce is filed, a summons is issued to notify the other spouse. In some instances, a temporary order is also requested at the same time as the petition.

For the most part, a temporary order will order each of the parties to take specific actions and/or refrain from doing certain things, until such time as the actual divorce trial can be heard by the court.9 After the defending spouse responds to the summons, and if both parties can agree, a divorce, with no minor children involved, may be granted within a few days. If minor children are involved, there may be a 90-180 day waiting period. If other circumstances, such as an emergency custody order or a contested divorce, are present the process may take much longer. In rare cases only one party must appear in court before a judge. At that time, the divorce may be granted. In several states, remarriage or cohabitation with a third party may be prohibited for a period of time, following the issuance of the final divorce decree.

Several approaches to divorce may be available in the judicial system, and with careful consideration, as well as, appropriate professional legal advice, you should be able to find the approach that is right for you.

A recent client, unhappy with receiving *"joint custody"* of his young daughter and having to pay over three million dollars *(above alimony and child support)* in a settlement to his ex-wife, enlisted my services. The goal was to set in motion an investigation to find enough information to file a motion to modify custody, from *"joint custody" to "sole custody".* It was the client's belief that his former spouse was not conducting herself to satisfy the best interest of the minor child.

During the one-year investigation we witnessed numerous events to support our client's concerns. We confirmed eight different and distinct romantic relationships in less than a year. The client's concern was that his former spouse's relationships were causing a lack of parental concern about the well-being of his minor child.

She would often choose not to be with the child, and leave her with a 15 year old babysitter. She frequently changed her visitations using "*business"* as the alleged reason, or giving no explanation whatsoever. After dropping off the child with either the father or the babysitter, she would meet up with a paramour for a night out on the town culminating in an all-night encounter at her residence.

Perhaps this behavior may not be a violation of the Court's order; however, preferring a *"night on the town"* and a *"sleepover"* may convince the Court that the child's best interest has become secondary, considering the dubious characteristics of this mother's choices.

Any parental activity, involving unknown acquaintances, which may affect the minor child(ren) may become a part of our investigation.

This may include individuals the parent dates, as well as those with whom they associate.

Our agency routinely conducts background checks on the parent's associates and/or paramours, including their civil and criminal records. Our investigation, in the above case, revealed that *four of the eight* men the former spouse dated had criminal records, including *DUI/DWI and abuse of a minor child.* The boyfriend, with the child abuse charges, had severely injured a former girlfriend's young daughter. Information such as this can result in a modification in primary custody as well as visitation.

The private investigator is frequently capable of gathering information, not readily accessible by the client or their attorney. Many times, this information may confirm suspicions, resulting in a successful outcome for the client's case.

In the same vein, the emotional stability of a parent is a very real concern. This may be especially true when the minor child*(ren)* will be spending time alone with each parent.

This brings to mind another particular case. I conducted an initial consultation with a young man, Jim, who had brought along his mother for support. He had a very strong suspicion that his wife, the mother of his only child, was having an extramarital affair and doing so in the presence of his minor child. He had no proof, but rather several of the signs a cheating heart tends to show. The spouse was supposedly a *"stay-at-home"* mother, so the client thought. Her days were relatively free to do whatever she wanted, with no fear of being discovered.

This could be a double betrayal, because if she was indeed having an affair, Jim believed it was with a mutual friend. Jim was obviously upset and nervous to be discussing such a private matter. As he related his concerns, I recognized immediately we were probably dealing with an adulteress. We set into motion a plan of action. Given that his young son was with his wife during most of the day, Jim leased a GPS tracker to be put on the vehicle his spouse was driving. The vehicle still belonged to and was registered only to our client.

During the course of our investigation, some of her activities began revealing what would ultimately be very important information. We captured on film all that she had denied, plus the identity of her paramour, which confirmed Jim's suspicion to be true. It was someone he knew very well. During many of these encounters, the minor child was present in the residence. This information was enough proof, for the client to consult his attorney and file a petition for divorce. In the petition, he requested sole custody of his son. When the court issued the final divorce decree, our client was awarded sole physical custody and child support.

During this investigation, relative and damaging information was discovered in the abandoned and discarded items retrieved from their residence. Notes were found in the trash regarding her feelings for another man, as well as, a note that caused concern regarding her emotional stability. She wrote of behavior patterns she continued to repeat in her process of looking for love. This information, along with the mother having the child present during her intimate encounters, ultimately became the primary ammunition used in trial. In fact, when the evidence was introduced into court, she relinquished custody voluntarily.

I would like to point out, that in the two previous cases, the information obtained was not an attempt to pass judgment on either of the individuals we investigated. As an investigator, I am hired to gather the true facts. This calls for observation and documentation of a person or person's activities that may affect the minor children, marital vows, marital assets and any possible criminal activity. As you can see, our choices and behaviors do not always paint a pretty picture. This is an important point to make, because if you are contemplating a divorce, your lifestyle during these proceedings and after the proceedings, could possibly be used against you in court.

Be conscious of the choices you make, how others might perceive them and how they might influence the court's ruling. Obtaining a fair and equitable settlement may require knowledge, to which many individuals do not have access. Issues like, the division of retirement assets and bonuses can be tricky. The specifics, regarding entitlement to these benefits, may be even trickier to the average man or woman.

You may live in a state that determines the value of retirement assets be split based on the actual date of separation, not divorce. The courts may direct you to divide the assets as of the date of separation. If your soon-to-be former spouse is about to get a bonus or retirement payout you may benefit from separating after the date of the bonus or payout. If you are not aware of this entitlement and your spouse is, it is possible there will be an attempt on the part of your spouse to keep you out of the loop and thereby, not have to share these assets.

Your solution may be to hire a competent attorney, to alert you to the legal ramifications in your particular state. This may be valuable to know *prior* to reaching the *"filing"* stage. During the *'pre-filing'* stage, using the private investigator may become an important bridge between truth *(facts)* and the way one spouse or the other perceives the truth.

On the flip side, a marital asset investigation may have nothing to do with an impending divorce. One of my cases involved a lady whose intentions were nowhere close to the divorce stage, but only curious, as to the distribution of marital assets. As you read the following case, you will realize why the client's PI fees were far less than the client's ultimate recovery of marital assets, when a divorce became inevitable.

A woman, twenty years younger than her very wealthy husband, engaged our services because she was concerned her spouse may be significantly reducing marital assets due to his excessive drinking. Her primary concern was to determine their financial situation involving their mutually owned company's assets.

When asked by the investigator if she suspected her husband of having an affair, she placed her finger girlishly on her cheek, turning it as she replied, *"Read my lips. There's no way he's having an affair. No one else would want him."*

A few weeks into the investigation of the subject, his regular routine was determined. The subject would leave the marital residence around 9 a.m. and proceed directly to his office, where he would stay for a couple of hours. He would then leave the office and proceed to his favorite downtown club. There he would spend two hours lunching and drinking *'vodka on the rocks.'* After his virtually liquid lunch he would return to his office and nap until around 3:45 p.m. He would then return to the same club where he had more *'vodka on the rocks,'* until 4:45 p.m. This routine became the blueprint of his activities. Occasionally, it varied to include driving his Mercedes, into a garage attached to a lovely home, in an upper-class neighborhood. This house belonged to a lady who was apparently "*kept*" very well. This was evident, considering she had recently acquired a brand new vehicle and a house full of very fine furniture. This appeared out of the ordinary considering the woman had recently quit her minimum wage job as a nurse's aid. Apparently, our subject had become reacquainted with this lady, who had once been an employee of a large company he had previously sold.

Approximately a year before our investigation began she advantageously bumped into him, during a time when she was struggling financially. The investigator uncovered information, within a relatively short period of time, confirming the client's concern that her husband's drinking might be diminishing their marital assets.

However, our client was extremely surprised to learn his drinking was not the only culprit. Obviously, the subject's former employee had become a factor, responsible for helping the husband spend a sizeable portion of the marital assets. Our client was certain no one else would want her man, but she failed to consider the seductive effect money could have on certain individuals in financial distress. This story illustrates the discovery of an unexpected paramour as well as the suspected reduction of marital assets, which were being disbursed to and through the previously unknown paramour.

The pursuit of truth is complex and may involve many aspects, impossible to predict, prior to beginning an investigation. While each case may consist of similar characteristics, the unique nature of each human being makes every case a new challenge. A spouse's unpredictable nature continues to perplex even the most seasoned wife or husband, causing one to question whether it is possible to *truly know* one another. The more specific question is, how a formerly trusted and loyal significant other will respond to temptation when coupled with a strained marital relationship. A strained relationship is always more susceptible to third party infiltration. In many cases, the third party is just the catalyst needed to take a person from mere dissatisfaction to divorce.

There is a type of struggling that some relationships enter into and after a time, either dissolve or repair. On a daily basis, in the private investigation business, this limbo is observed. However, more often than not, a third party has entered into the picture. Another case history describes such a situation.

A well-respected research doctor, named Nancy, retained our agency's services, to find out if her husband, Stan, also a research doctor working in the same department as Nancy, was having an affair with another out-of-state female doctor and colleague. Prior to retaining our agency, Nancy's suspicions led her to confront both her husband and Stephanie, the suspected paramour. They both vehemently denied any affair whatsoever.

Nancy had entertained Stephanie; in fact, Stephanie and her husband had stayed overnight in the client's home on several different occasions. During Stephanie's visits, Nancy's husband wined and dined Stephanie late into the night, using the pretense he was attempting to woo her into accepting a position, within their local department.

On one of Stephanie's visits, Nancy suspected (based on missing tablets of Viagra) that her husband "wooed" Stephanie into the guest bedroom of their home, which was directly above the bedroom Nancy and Stan shared.

Stan continued giving Nancy mixed signals about their relationship. While trying to convince her there was nothing extramarital going on, Stan even told Nancy the woman in question might be gay. He went on to suggest he would enjoy watching the two of them *(his wife and Stephanie)* have sex together. Nancy began to describe other behaviors she had noticed over the past few months. As we conversed, it became evident to me Stan was the perfect model for "The Signs of a Cheating Heart." Nancy hired our agency a few days prior to Stephanie's next visit. Our investigators were ready when Stephanie arrived at the local airport.

Stan met Stephanie with a gentle hug at the baggage claim area, retrieved her luggage, and proceeded to his vehicle, which was waiting in the short-term airport parking area. Once in the vehicle, our camera lens captured several passionate kisses, hugs and playful gesturing of two people totally obsessed with each other.

During Stephanie's stay, the couple's activities, captured on film, provided the necessary information for Nancy to begin to comprehend her husband's actions. At Nancy's request, we continued to work on the case for several months, stockpiling information. Stan's actions and our documentation were making the case for our client's attorney. Stan seemed to believe he was invincible. His wife's intelligence and her female intuition were paying off. Perhaps he thought mid-life somehow shielded him from the all-seeing eye.

Stan was very smug, condescending and righteous all the way to the end. Stan had manipulated favor with the head of their department and subtly slandered Nancy's character around the research laboratory. This was very upsetting for Nancy. If not for the loads of information to the contrary, Nancy could have been perceived by her colleagues as a psychotic, insecure and suspicious wife. She was even afraid she was going to find herself on the unemployment line. Her career was now at stake, all because her husband could not admit his infidelity and unfaithfulness. It was not until Stan's attorney inquired about the information against his client that Stan backed down. Prior to that point, Stan continued to deny any wrongdoing. Suddenly, his smugness began to diminish. Nancy succeeded in the courtroom and today her career flourishes, although the experience was heartbreaking. Imagine the outcome had we not been in her corner.

I have only skimmed the surface where issues of divorce are concerned. The scenarios are endless. While the majority of divorces are mostly amicable, there are plenty that require a more in-depth effort, to resolution. Your chances for a fair and equitable outcome, in a divorce-related situation, may be far more likely when the services of a competent private investigator are engaged. The primary reason most clients retain our services is suspicion of infidelity. Knowing the signs of a cheating spouse may buffer your breaking heart, as your life turns into lyrics from the familiar country and western song, "Your Cheating Heart Will Tell on You."

Four

Your Cheating Heart Will Tell On You

In an open and fairly well lit bar, in the middle of the afternoon, a couple challenged each other in a game of pool. The moderately populated bar very easily displayed the couple. From a stranger's point of view, the man and woman seemed as if they were obviously in love and excited to be with each other. The gold bands worn on their left hands further confirmed this. However, the gold bands did not tell the whole story – they were both married, just not to each other.

Most private investigators have probably compiled a list of *cheating signs* received from their clients, who suspect their spouse is cheating. If an actual list was not made, a mental inventory is checked off each time this type of case is described. These signs are so commonly articulated, during the initial consultation, that the investigator knows what the client is going to say before he or she says it. However, the client is usually not aware of these warning signs or how universal they are. The signs may not be obvious to the victim *until* the betrayed is in the position to look back upon the experience.

The following list is not comprehensive, but even with different vocabulary, the content remains the same. Take a moment to examine the list compiled by our office, which is based on descriptions involving numerous infidelity cases, seen over the years. Should any, or all, of the signs strike a chord with you, you may find out your mate, partner or significant other is cheating on you. If you do not recognize any of these signs, thank your lucky stars, tuck the knowledge away and hope you never have to call upon it again. Finally, if you see yourself in the behaviors listed below, realize that while your spouse may not yet be aware of your actions, these well-known signs may catch up with you eventually.

A recent "Primetime Live" poll indicates that sixteen percent of adults polled admit to cheating. Males still lead in the area of extramarital activities by twenty-one percent, compared to eleven percent of the women.10 This is echoed in an original report by NBC's "20/20" news story entitled "SEX: Myths, Lies and Straight Talk." The question asked, "Are women naturally more monogamous than men?" Based upon expert data, provided by one private investigator's business, men appear to be cheating twice as much as women. This is based on who is actually hiring the investigator and since, in this poll, more women retained the services of a private investigator than did men, it was determined men are cheating more than women.11

Our agency has consistently, over the last ten years, had an almost equal, 50/50 split, in male and female clients requesting our services.

SIGNS OF A CHEATING HEART

•Claims to be working a lot of overtime.
•Is no longer wearing a wedding ring.
•Says "I just need some space."
•Accuses the other spouse of being "crazy."
•Adds unexplained additional mileage on vehicle.
•Purchases new and attractive under garments.
•Develops a sudden interest in 'working out' or 'tanning salons'.
•Becomes interested in trying new or bizarre things sexually.
•Becomes less attentive in family issues and to you.
•Has more cash on hand than usual.
•Hangs out with new friends and/or new locations.
•Has consistent smells of perfume, cologne, or alcohol.
•Use of ATM machines in new or unexplained locations.
•Hides cell-phone bills, mailing to the office or a P.O. Box.
•Is no longer interested in sex or the other person's needs.
•Receives suspicious or 'coded' voice messages or text messages.
•Begins a sudden increase in time away from home.
•Is easily distracted and is daydreaming.
•Is not returning your phone calls in a timely fashion.
•Asks about your schedule more than usual
•Gets his or her laundry done independently.
•Uses more Viagra or other new prescription drugs.
•Pays more attention to clothes and accessories.
•Has unexplained receipts or personal effects in wallet or purse.
•Has unexplained payments or withdrawals on bank statement.
•Gas or credit card receipts from inconsistent locations.
•Makes unusually short or long phone calls.
•Visits uncommon sites on the internet.
•Gets odd or peculiar e-mail messages.
•Becomes nervous/agitated when on the phone or computer.
•Puts new passwords on cell phone, email and computer.
•Gets calls from 'blocked' or 'unidentified' numbers.
•Uses the Internet, email, and instant messaging excessively.

This is just one cultural sampling. The investigator interviewed for this story believes women are rapidly catching up in this area. Our agency's recent statistics, in this area, support the above findings, but not quite to the degree already reported. Sixty percent of our infidelity cases are women who suspect their spouse or significant other of cheating. That leaves forty percent to the men, which creates a smaller gap between the sexes and confirms the belief that women are on the rise in the infidelity arena. It is important to point out again, that these statistics are based on which sex is doing the hiring, and does not include conclusive data, regarding findings of guilt or other factors such as whether or not the client was also cheating at the time services were retained.

In an article, "Office Affairs" by Peggy Vaughan, she addresses the question of why more women are having office affairs today than in the past.12 It does not take a rocket scientist to figure it out, but most people do not entertain these questions until faced with an article or television news story. Ms. Vaughan simply points out the preoccupation our society has with sex and the sexually charged and commercialized innuendo created by the media. This increases the expectation of sex in the office and since more women are in the workforce than ever before, more women are subject to having affairs. She indicates two situations men have always been exposed to – time spent with co-workers in the office and travel in conjunction with their jobs – now tempt women as well. Some might find the recent exposé *"To Love, Honor and Betray: The Secret Lives of Suburban Wives,"* by Stephanie Gertler, a bit disturbing, perhaps due to the status to which we exalt wives and mothers. The report, regarding Gertler's book, comes on the heels of the highly popular television drama/comedy, *"Desperate Housewives"* that seems to exemplify the sexually charged state of our society.

According to Gertler, all twenty-six married women, described in her book, are either *"cheating on their husbands, have already cheated, or are constantly struggling with their loyalties and emotions as they consider cheating."13* Whatever the reason or motivation, businesses like ours are seeing the gap between the sexes rapidly closing, bringing equality to all human beings across the board.

Although infidelity is the "bread and butter" of our business, from a moral and ethical standpoint, we feel duty-bound to reiterate, *"We do not promote or condone cheating."* This is never an acceptable alternative to an honest and responsible effort to maintain a committed relationship. However, infidelity continues to top the list of reasons why couples divorce; therefore, agencies like ours will continue to shine light on the truth for those who hire us.

In the private investigation business, we see the dark side of humanity. We see what most people hide from the rest of the world -- their bosses, co-workers, friends, family members and their spouse or significant other. In hiding their secrets from the world, they attempt to hollow out a cocoon-like existence, where they feel their double-life is not detectable. This is illustrated in the story that began this chapter, which I will now continue.

The two private investigators, playing pool next to the *"married, but-not-to-each-other"* couple, looked, to the onlookers in the bar, like the normal Friday-after-work crowd. There are so many parallel dimensions in society, invisible corridors we all walk within. The unsuspecting eye sees the bar as a room filled with people drinking, talking and smoking. But the private investigator sees beyond the obvious.

The couple related playfully to one another as if they were the only people in the room or as if they were hiding behind an invisible cloak. The private investigators watched, as an adulterous affair was developed, only a couple of miles from where the man resided, in the town he and his family call home.

From the pool table, the couple left the bar with a false sense of security, believing an invisible cloak surrounded them. His car was parked in the first space next to the bar, right outside the window of the poolroom.

As they were paying their tab and preparing to leave the club, the nonobservant couple failed to notice the investigators, who were exiting ahead of them. The investigators proceeded directly to a vehicle parked outside where a surveillance camera was poised and ready to record.

As the couple left the club, they were caught on tape leaving hand-in-hand, laughing and holding one another intimately. The action in the *spouse's vehicle,* with the female sitting across our client's husband's lap dissolved any remaining doubt.

For our client, this proof erased the self-doubt she had developed over the past few months. With her spouse's constant lying and his attempts to convince her she was crazy and exceedingly jealous, the thought of him having an affair had basically vanished from her mind.

Even when suspicion begins to creep into the thoughts of the betrayed, denial enables the betrayer to continue the dance of deceit, as is evident in this case, where the spouse seemingly had no thought of being caught.

Private investigators see what others either do not notice or wish to avoid. Through covert surveillance, which is most often a lonely and tiring job, the investigator observes the subject or subjects, when their guard is down. By profession, the investigator blends into the environment, becoming the name everyone knows at the local bar or someone who works out next to you at the gym, or just another diner at your favorite restaurant.

The investigator may be found sitting behind darkly tinted windows, in a *"neighborhood friendly"* vehicle, photographing and documenting a secret rendezvous thought to be concealed from the rest of the world. Sure, it's obvious to the investigator what is going on but the rest of the world is seeing it without realizing a "crime of the heart" is being committed. We all have a voice inside that alerts us to danger and discrepancies in our lives. A subconscious recorder is collecting everything that is seen, heard and felt. Our subconscious knows when things are *out of order,* long before it enters our consciousness. Trusting your instinct and intuition is a learned behavior. Although it is difficult to keep emotions intact in matters of the heart, acting on these instincts should be done very carefully and with much thought. This is another reason a qualified private investigator is one of your best resources during your emotional battle.

Trust is a fundamental component of a loving partnership. However, as long as mankind has free will, betrayal is a fundamental potential in any relationship. The adulterer is, more often than not, so involved with their affair, they are unaware of the subtle shifts in their behavior. Since deception is a deviant art, unconscious patterns become visible. A web of lies continues to be spun throughout the adulterated relationship. Being aware of signs and trusting your instinct could keep you out of a downwardly spiraling emotional roller coaster ride.

Infidelity is non-discriminatory. It befriends the highly educated, successful professional, the middle-class, the blue-collar and the poverty stricken. No class is affair-proof.

Finding yourself in a suspicious situation is a heart-wrenching experience. If you recognize any of the signs listed in this chapter, chances are you may be caught in a "web of infidelity". Learning the truth about your situation may put you on the path to a private investigation agency and/or an attorney. If this path turns into the road to divorce, preparation and precautions should be addressed as early as possible.

Five

Precautions to Take When Contemplating a Divorce

To anyone on the outside looking in, this thirty year marriage seemed perfect. In fact, it seemed ideal to one of the insiders. However, a small, relatively undetectable crack had quietly begun to widen and spread down the length of their marriage. Ironically, Joan's husband began telling her she was cracking up; at about the same time the fractured shell of their marriage became noticeable.

It never occurred to Joan that, by attacking her mental health, he was diverting the attention from himself to her. Losing her mind was easier to believe than the string of reality she began to pull at, which unraveled into an unexpected truth, revealing betrayal and deceit. She had, blindly, put her trust and faith in her husband's leadership for the past three decades, and now, it turns out, she has been kept in the dark regarding almost every aspect of their life. They have been living his version of their life, with him telling her only what he wants her to know, which includes vague knowledge about their finances and how they are generated. It's obvious he didn't want her to know about his mistress either.

One of the most traumatic events to occur in a person's life is the downfall of a marriage. Divorce is a loss, regardless of who initiates it, and should be treated as such. The process of recovery, from such a life-changing experience, is best begun at the onset.

Thoughtful steps might include: enlisting emotional support from family and friends, psychological support from a counselor or clergy member and physical activity for taking extra care of your health. Your lifestyle and behavior choices may be more closely scrutinized during the divorce process. This includes the time before, during and after. While you are taking the necessary steps to care for yourself, the manner in which you do so should be considered. While you may feel compelled to cry in a beer at your local pub or seek solace in the arms of a new beau, be very careful how you go about it. Remember the story of the woman who, after divorcing her husband, began a string of romances with somewhat shady characters. While, as far as we know, she was doing nothing illegal, she could be perceived as being more interested in spending time with various men, than with her daughter. In a custody battle, this type of behavior could be detrimental to the mother's case.

Another area, best tackled at the onset, involves protecting yourself financially. It is difficult enough to believe your marriage is dissolving, much less that the person you trusted most is capable of causing you fiscal and lifestyle harm. For this reason, it is in your best interest to take certain precautions, when a divorce looms ahead.

Leave No Paper Trail

Although you may be looking for paper trails and clues of your spouse's actions, bear in mind, that at some point during the divorce process, through discovery or subpoena, your paper trail may be uncovered as well. Protect yourself by using payments of cash and/or your own personal credit card, which is unknown to the other party. You should also be aware of your activity on the cell phone, as well as residential and office phones. Be certain you are talking only to individuals, who have an interest in your well-being and would not be detrimental to you, if called as a witness.

Many instances of a written diary or recorded account of day-to-day actions have been brought into play when they become known or located by the other party.

How to Discretely Get Money to Pay an Attorney or PI

Keep in mind, the suggestions here are only suggestions and should not be misconstrued as legal advice. You should consult with your attorney prior to using any of these recommendations.

Consider certain items you may be able to discreetly purchase, such as clothing, household items, artwork or anything you can buy on a joint credit card or your spouse's credit card, which can later be returned to the store for credit. At the time the credit is issued, request a gift certificate in the amount of the credit. For example, if you buy a party dress for Christmas or New Year's, you can purchase the dress and then return it, get the credit and wear something already hanging in your closet. If you're in charge of paying the bills on the credit card purchases, consider paying the balance but adding a few hundred dollars to the account giving you a credit balance. Request gift certificates for the credit balance and then retain those gift certificates for purchases made after your divorce. Merchants, such as Home Depot, Dillard's, JC Penney's, and your dry cleaners are various places where you could pre-pay an additional amount to use for your future benefit.

When purchasing staples such as food and clothing, request that you be able to write the check for extra cash at the time of the purchase, reserving that cash for future needs and discreet purchases after the divorce. You may also want to consider the condition of the vehicle you will be left with, and make certain you have new tires, brakes and the various upkeep items on the vehicle. Otherwise, that could be your responsibility after the divorce. Make certain everything is in top-notch condition at the time you file for divorce. You may even want to consider suggesting to your spouse, that you need a new vehicle as the other one doesn't seem safe for your family.

You should consider the remaining debt on anything that's purchased, such as your vehicle, realizing that it could possibly become your responsibility to pay the balance out of the proceeds of your alimony or portion of the marital estate.

Again, your attorney would be the proper person, from whom to get concrete advice, as to how to handle this type of transaction. At the time of your initial interview with the investigating agency, other suggestions may be made from time to time that will not be mentioned between the covers of this book. By taking certain steps, you may avoid seeing your former spouse wining and dining in the finest places and driving a fine vehicle, while you are left with little, or nothing, for day-to-day expenses. This could be especially true during the temporary order period, should the court give you less than adequate temporary support.

Copy ALL Documentation

When you suspect your marriage may be heading down the path of divorce, make sure you have a copy of all original documentation. This includes, but not limited to, bank accounts, savings accounts, retirement funds, investments, insurance policies, mortgages and Federal and State Income Tax documents.

Once a divorce is filed, it may become more difficult to obtain the documents from your spouse. These documents may only be obtained by subpoena or discovery if the spouse tries to be difficult. If at all possible, you should very discreetly and without the other party's knowledge, obtain a copy of everything that would relate to you and your spouse's financial condition. You may want to return the documents to their original location to avoid any suspicion you are actually copying the documents. As you acquire these copied documents, place them in a secure location, preferably outside the marital residence or any place where your spouse or significant other may have access.

You may also want to consider your, soon to be, ex-spouse's office as a place to obtain copies of phone records, tax returns, business accounts and items which you may not have easy access to after your divorce petition has been filed. It is quite common for spouses to change the locks, prepare false or inaccurate documents or advise all personnel to avoid allowing you to have access to certain files that may be pertinent to the divorce. You may want to consider having a forensic team clone and review any computers you have legal access to, prior to a petition being filed. The cloning process should take no more than two to three hours per computer, and many times, less time than that. Searching for computerized documents and files can be done at a later date as the process develops. The purpose is to merely get your hands on items that can be used by your attorney, to backup and/or confirm the financial condition of the marital estate you have accumulated with your spouse.

When searching for certain documents, in particular those in the office of your spouse, you may want to consider doing it after hours, on holidays or weekends, when the other party would not readily be close to the office, or when your actions will not be observed. Again, be sure anything you do is done in a legally acceptable manner. Be sure to note account numbers and dates of opening and closing of accounts.

Another important area of documentation, that could prove valuable, would be any type of purchase, where a loan application has been filled out, whether it is for a home or auto. It is quite common, for the applicant of a loan, to exaggerate their income and assets, showing their financial condition in the best possible light for the financial institution to approve the loan. At a later date, during the divorce process, when the party uses different figures that lower the amount of their income and net worth, your attorney will have documentation to use to contradict and confirm the parties are being less than truthful.

Separate Bank Accounts

You may want to consider opening a separate checking and/or savings account. Many assets may be frozen by the temporary order and removing funds from accounts may become restricted, therefore you may want to withdraw money prior to the filing of a divorce.

Opening a separate account from your spouse may be advised in order to have some avenue of accumulating and/or disbursing funds, when the need arises. This will be discussed in greater detail, during your personal interview with the investigator.

Remember, these are only ideas for you to *consider.* We strongly advise you to seek the advice of your attorney.

Obtain a Safety Deposit Box

A safety deposit box is necessary for the safe keeping of documentation and other important information. To open a safety deposit box is no more difficult than to open a bank account. Many people maintain a safety deposit box to secure important documentation during the course of a divorce.

Obtain a Post Office Box

When couples are going through a divorce or separation, the party who is no longer living in the residence, has been known to go by the residence, when it is known the spouse is not home, to check the mail and read or see what mail or correspondence is being received. For this reason, you may want to consider getting a separate post office box. To keep correspondence between you and other parties private, a post office box will come in handy. In some cities, companies lease post office boxes that appear to be a house and street address, so you can get around the "P.O. Box not accepted" on various applications.

Access and Analyze Emails and Cell Phones

You should *check the statutes within your state,* regarding computer fraud and computer privacy, prior to accessing or reading any of your spouse's emails that may be on the computer. *This should be discussed in detail with your attorney to protect you from any type of computer crime.* Be certain you do not do anything that could be used against you or could result in criminal charges or allegations against you. Copies of cell phone records can be researched to determine with whom your spouse has been in contact. If indiscretions are found, these records can be subpoenaed by your attorney and legally presented in court. The Internet is another area to obtain information of an affair. If your spouse's email is not password protected and you access your spouse's email account, it may be apparent in the saved and new files, if he or she is corresponding with a third party to your marriage. Be certain you do not violate any state or federal laws in this process.

If the email address is all you have, an investigator may be able to attract your spouse into forming an online relationship. This tactic, on occasions, has met with great success. In fact, we have had long-term correspondence with a suspected philandering spouse. Using an alias screen name we have uncovered the kind of personal information exchanged late at night within a budding romance.

By allowing your investigator to handle the pretext messaging with the wayward spouse, you may be able to use certain excerpts or information, obtained by the investigator, in the courtroom rather than attempting to do anything that is forbidden by the computer crime statutes in your state.

Be Careful What Drugs are in Your Medicine Cabinet

If one spouse convinces the other they need psychological help, accusing them of being crazy, encouraging them to seek help, beware of how this might affect your divorce or custody. If you begin seeing a therapist, who prescribes anti-depressants and you

Instant:
Should be nice =)
Call me...
can I see you?...
have to Work lat
sorry
5:30
Private Call...
Answer
silent

are trying to gain custody of your children, you may be asked, under oath, if you are taking any mind-altering drugs. Manipulation is a common tactic used by wayward spouse's to obtain custody of their children. Again, discuss this openly with your attorney.

Prior to filing for divorce, you may want to request your pharmacist give you a printout of your family's drug purchases. You may discover information of which you are unaware or may confirm what you already suspect. Either way, this information may be a piece of information that will help your case. Obtaining the information may be as simple as requesting your pharmacy to provide you with the records. This is fairly common for purposes such as income tax filing. However, after filing for a divorce, a subpoena may be necessary and obtaining medical records are not always forthcoming if the other side objects to the request.

Abandoned and Discarded Items

The other side of the garbage issue applies to anyone contemplating divorce. The bottom line is this: Do not throw away anything you do not want to become public knowledge. Always assume your spouse may also have hired a private investigator. The contents of your garbage canister or dumpster could show up in court and become a determining factor in the outcome of your case. We always caution our clients to keep their trash very sterile – generic – don't throw away medicine bottles, bank statements, checks, receipts, credit card statements, envelopes with return addresses, food, liquor bottles, etc. There is no expectation of privacy, once you leave your trash receptacle by the curb. The same type of information used against your spouse could also be used against you if you are not careful.

There are many issues to consider when filing for what you believe will be a mutually agreed upon and amicable divorce. When you begin to add other factors, such as deceit and betrayal, the issues become numerous, adding to an already stressful event. The best strategy for any significant change in your life is to *be prepared and to have a plan.* The primary reason for writing this book is to pass along knowledge I have collected over the years in hopes it will benefit someone else. The legal side of the divorce process is often new territory for most people encountering divorce, not to mention the emotional aspects involved in dissolving a marital relationship can be the biggest event in one's life. It is easy to forget the possible ramifications of your actions, whether past, present or future, when it comes to the outcome of a divorce.

Private investigators and divorce attorneys are acutely aware of the many precautions mentioned in this chapter, while most individuals are not. These precautions rarely enter into the average person's mind but may play a significant role in divorce and child custody litigation. Divorce cases and custody cases commonly go hand in hand; therefore, many of the suggestions in this book will apply to both, and in some instances be crucial to the outcome of a case.

Six

The Role of a PI in Custody Suits

Five years after a one-night stand, Richard woke up on the wrong side of a paternity suit. The woman had long since faded from his memory. It was difficult to fathom a child having been born out of such an unremarkable and transitory encounter. However, if a child, his child, did exist, on this earth as his living, breathing legacy, he would gladly pay the admission fee to be a part of his or her life.

The information a private investigator can bring to a divorce case is just as important to a custody case and in some ways, possibly more so, considering the welfare of a minor child is at stake. While the above excerpt is from an unusual custody campaign, the remainder of the story illuminates the effectiveness of a private investigation. In the vast majority of paternity suits, the mother is usually the plaintiff and usually wins, but if there is to be an exception, a private investigator will likely be involved. Let us continue with Richard's case as an example.

Richard came from New England to study Air Traffic Control with the Federal Aviation Administration (FAA) in Oklahoma City. He was single and had been for many years. While in school, he dated a couple of women, but did not have time to pursue a serious relationship due to his studies. He did, however, have a one-night stand with a woman he met at a party prior to leaving Oklahoma for the next phase of his training.

Five years later a paternity suit was filed against him claiming he was the father of a five-year-old girl living in Oklahoma City. Her mother was the woman with whom he had spent one night while in FAA school. Richard was being sued for past and future child support for a child he had no idea even existed. If the child were indeed his, he would gladly fulfill his financial obligation but also wanted to provide more than just financial support. He wanted to meet the child and realize all fatherly responsibilities possible. The court ordered him to pay back child support and granted him standard visitation rights.

However, when he would attempt to visit his child, the mother, using various excuses, kept him from seeing the child. Each time he tried to uphold his end of the visitation arrangements, his time and money traveling to Oklahoma from New England were continuously wasted. At this point, he decided that if he were going to pay this kind of support and not get to see his child he would file a motion for full custody. Obviously, he would have a pretty tough battle on his hands, having not lived with the child or even seen the child during the past five years. That is when he hired a competent attorney and our investigative agency.

We began investigating the woman immediately and learned many fascinating facts. She was 32 years old and supported herself as a tarot card reader, doing the readings out of her lower income apartment. She was described as an FAA groupie who had been involved with numerous men from the FAA Training Center. We also discovered she had terminated three previous pregnancies. The nature of her "work" gave us the perfect pretext to begin our investigation in a very up close and personal manner.

On a warm Saturday afternoon, we sent a female undercover investigator to the woman's apartment to have her cards read. When the investigator arrived for the reading, other investigators were stationed outside with covert cameras poised toward the apartment and surrounding area. The subject's apartment was located in a large apartment community, in a less desirable area of town where crime was somewhat epidemic. When the undercover investigator was ushered inside for the reading, the little girl was ushered out the door and told to stay outside and play during the reading. Inside, the apartment was dark with numerous candles aglow, and the musky stench of incense hung in the air.

During the *hour and a half* reading, the subject's daughter was observed running around the apartment complex with no supervision whatsoever. She was observed running in and out of one particular apartment occupied by three young men. They were all sitting around in their underwear, drinking alcoholic beverages. The little girl wandered throughout the sizable complex, going as far as five buildings away from her apartment. Anything could have happened to her during this period of time.

The investigator returned on three different occasions for more readings. This allowed for us to accumulate approximately five hours of video showing the little girl wandering around the apartment

4B

complex, falling and hurting herself and being comforted by total strangers and others in the apartment complex. Additionally, through information gathered from the abandoned and discarded items, we learned the mother was a regular user of marijuana and prescription drugs. After a six-month investigation of the woman's activities, and her parenting *(or non-parenting)* skills, the client's attorney filed a motion to modify custody; in fact, our client filed for sole custody. The motion contained a request for child support and everything else that full custody implies. The case went to trial using the information we had produced. The information, along with the exemplary character of the father, extracted a resounding victory. The judge awarded full custody to Richard and ordered the mother to pay child support. Today, the child continues to live happily with her father and is an A+ student.

The divorce process, between two adults is as unique as the marriage itself, as well as the adults involved. There is no perfect way to approach a divorce. However, there is a better way to separate and it does not include hand-to-hand, in-the-trenches combat. Children are at the heart of any custody battle and we encourage an amicable dissolution of the marital contract, assuming there are no alternatives. Although there is probably some bitterness between you and your spouse, it should not be inflicted upon your children. The manner in which you involve and relate with your children during the divorce process is based on common sense; however, the following suggestions regarding conduct offered by the Oklahoma Bar Association may be helpful.

1. Do not poison your child's mind against the opposite parent.
2. Do not expose your children to any romantic involvements.
3. Do not argue with the other parent during visitation exchanges.
4. Do not visit your children if you have been drinking.
5. Do not visit your children at unreasonable hours.
6. Notify your spouse immediately if you are unable to keep your visitation.
7. Do not make extravagant promises to your children.
8. Always work for the spiritual well-being, health, happiness and safety of your children.

The child has not asked for his or her life to be turned upside down and wants more than anything in the world to have both parents under the same roof. This is a life-changing event for your child and, using common sense and making good choices with your child's best interest in mind, will ease the transition.

Although it is impossible to escape the effects divorce has on children, studies have shown that staying in an unhappy marriage for the children's benefit actually does more damage to those you think you are protecting. Consequently, staying in a negative situation is not the answer. Once you have determined divorce is the only answer, the number one consideration should be the welfare of the child(ren). The best possible scenario for the child is for both parents to be responsible for raising the child and for both to actively participate in the child's life; however, awarding sole custody continues to be the norm in many states. You should discuss with your attorney the pros and cons of sole versus joint custody which, depending on the relationship and the quality of life your children would have under each of these possibilities. Your attorney can advise you as to what to expect and how to decide what is best for your children, as well as standard and custom visitation schedules. The demeanor and manner in which the divorcing couple relates to each other and their compatibility and lifestyle can determine part of this.

Statistics from the 1997 U.S. Census Current Population Survey and the National Center for Health Statistics show that in sixty-nine percent of child custody cases, the mother was awarded sole custody. Of these cases, nine percent were awarded to the father and twenty-two percent were awarded joint custody.14

Since 1970, the argument for joint custody has been picking up steam. The first joint custody statute was passed in Indiana in 1973 and now all 50 states recognize this option. In fact, shared parenting is the preference in 30 states and the District of Columbia.15

According to the Children's Rights Council Web site, Supreme Court decisions have found that "the interest of parents in their relationship with their children is sufficiently fundamental to come within the finite class of liberty interests protected by the Fourteenth Amendment." Because a fundamental right cannot be denied without a compelling state interest that cannot be achieved by any less restrictive means, some legal scholars believe, in the absence of abuse or neglect, parents have a right to both legal and physical joint custody.16

The key words here are "in the absence of abuse or neglect." While I am not a judge in these matters, the question of a parent's character or behavior could be construed as a form of abuse or neglect. At the very least, it may cause rightful concern. There are instances when a spouse becomes unrecognizable, due to a secret double life that might include an addiction or infidelity. Bad choices may not make the person a bad parent, but the concern is legitimate, when a child is involved.

Janet, a very successful and highly respected professional, fell in love with and married Joe, a less financially secure partner. Within a couple of years their only child was born. Several years into the marriage, due to his current behavior and attitude toward Janet, Joe became unrecognizable to her. He no longer even seemed like the same man with whom she had fallen in love. After a while she began to suspect he was having an affair and Janet hired our agency to find out the truth. Once our initial investigation confirmed the hard, cold facts of an affair, it was enough to prompt Janet to file for a divorce. However, other information made the fight for sole custody inevitable.

Joe was an average looking but charismatic man with little, or no ambition. The double life he led was very similar to many other cheating husbands; however, an excessive amount of pornography was found hidden in the family's garage and on the family computer.

The computer, also being used by their 7-year-old daughter, was not password protected. This made viewing of hardcore pornography easily and readily available, to the child even if it happened by accident. While no mother or father may want to deny their child the right to a relationship with "both" parents, discovering these dark details raised serious concern about the welfare of their only child, while in the care of her soon-to-be-ex-husband. Combine this knowledge with mimed threats such as gestures using a finger to slice across her throat and suddenly, Janet's highest priority became protecting herself and her child.

In this case Joe's extramarital activities, while in the presence of his minor child, took precedence over his duties as a parent. His choices may not automatically make him a bad parent, but they were certainly a bad example for their young daughter.

Another example of parental anxiety regarding child custody was revealed in another case involving extramarital relations and an obsession for pornography. Sandy, a young mother, thought she was living a dream life – loving husband and spiritual leader; three young, beautiful children; a comfortable home; and extras like a ski lodge in Colorado and a cabin on the lake. Because of their family commitment to their church, it took Sandy much longer for the warning signs to register. When Sandy was finally confronted with the reality of a possible affair, it felt like a firm, large hand had slapped across her still youthful face. The sting of her spouse's possible affair resonated for days in Sandy's mind. To make matters even worse, all the clues were leading to a young neighbor girl – not a woman, a girl of fifteen. A relationship with a minor, apparently being condoned by the girl's parents, had been going on right under Sandy's nose, yet she had no proof, only suspicion. Sandy contacted our agency for the purpose of documenting the truth even though she knew she might not have the stomach to handle it. Sandy needed an objective, non-biased, third party opinion, to confirm or put to rest her fears and suspicions. In her mind, all the circumstances were beyond her realm of comprehension and control. After confirming the affair with the young girl, we thought it necessary to suggest to the client, she have a forensic computer technician take a look at their computer. To no one's surprise, the computer technician found a huge amount of pornography, but the huge number of files found – over 3,500 – was astounding.

This may be a good time to interject information regarding an epidemic becoming prevalent in our society. ABC's news magazine "20/20" recently reported on the damaging effects cyber porn is having on Internet users.17 The new drug of choice flows freely (unless it is certain hardcore, then it may cost from $50 to thousands a month) and can become addictive. According to a New York-based sex therapist, Doris Hayden, "Like any addiction, it's progressive. Unless the person goes for help, it gets worse."

As quoted in Lynn Sherr's report, "Experts say there are hundreds of thousands of men out there, addicted to cyber porn, many of whom say that sex in cyberspace is the most intense sexual experience, ever." Considering this, it is not surprising that two cases, involving cyber porn, were referred to our office during the same window of time. This dangerous and growing addiction is breaking up families across the nation. Like any other addiction, it may have a profound effect on your custody rights as a parent in a court of law.

An Oklahoma judge ruled against overnight visitations for Mark and his young daughter. Mark was the subject of an investigation, conducted for a client, who wanted a divorce, but wanted sole custody of their daughter. Our client's number one reason for wanting a divorce and custody was the fact that Mark was an alcoholic and our client questioned his ability to properly care for their young daughter alone. Mark, of course, claimed to be in therapy for his addiction to pornography and claimed to have completely stopped drinking.

Through our usual investigative process, we discovered Mark had not changed his habits. We found bag after bag of empty alcohol containers in his trash over the period of the investigation. Photographs of the information were entered into the attorney's information binder. During the trial, Mark was answering, under oath, all questions pertaining to his alcohol abuse. He again proclaimed he had stopped drinking and was seeking therapy for his addiction to pornography. His attorney even produced invoices from therapists to document and substantiate Mark's claim.

After Mark's testimony, my client's attorney requested the court grant permission to call another witness, as a rebuttal witness to Mark's testimony. The court agreed. I took the stand and identified all the pornographic photographs and alcohol containers as having come from Mark's curbside garbage canister.

During the course of my testimony, Mark sat with his head down, his demeanor appearing deflated. The judge ruled quickly for my client to have sole custody, with the ex-husband having only minimal "supervised" visitation. Had there not been someone in her corner, the outcome could have been much different.

The objective is not to exclude or deny a deserving parent from the life of his child; however, a good parent must take every precaution to safeguard the best interest of the child. In the cases just mentioned, the welfare of the child was the primary concern. Unfortunately, these situations can produce combative behavior between the adults, leaving the child in a painful position.

Our office investigated another case, involving divorce, where custody was the major issue. Both parties seemed to be upstanding, honorable, moral and respected members of the community. Going into this investigation, we believed our client's efforts to obtain full custody would be more difficult, considering each of their "apparent" lack of flaws. However, during the course of the investigation, this flawless subject was just not adding up. On one occasion, the wife mentioned a very young man (barely out of his teens) who lived in her neighborhood. This young man and our client's spouse had become very close. The client then noticed that shortly after her spouse moved out of the marital residence, this young man, who had no apparent means of financial support, purchased a brand new luxury sports car. She believed, maybe, the young man played into the present circumstances of her marriage.

Her intuition was sending red flags. Something was just not right. After beginning surveillance of the subject's fashionable residence, with attached four-car garage, a significant development occurred. One evening about dusk, a young man, driving a red luxury sports car arrived. He appeared to have a garage door opener and backed into the subject's garage. As the garage door was closing, I could see the young man enter the house.

As the sun disappeared into the night sky, we watched the lights in the house, as they led us from room to room. The light trail began in the living room, leaving darkness behind as it moved from one room to another, ending in the master bedroom suite. Not long after the bedroom became illuminated, the lights dimmed, leaving what goes on behind closed doors to the imagination. Nine hours had passed from the time the young man in the sports car arrived until he drove his sports car out of the garage and disappeared into the night. By documenting this event, using video, as well as still photography, we had more than enough information to prevail in our client receiving full custody.

The subject was adamant. He did not want his homosexual encounters brought out in the public forum of the courtroom. He then quickly agreed to relinquish custody and pay more than ample child support, if the private investigator be stricken from the witness list and our client's attorney would agree not to put the related photographs into evidence.

In virtually every divorce/custody case our office has investigated, our services have played a part in the outcome of each case; sometimes a small part, often times a very large part. Not every divorce needs a private investigator, but those that do will also need a competent attorney, who not only endorses our work but also knows how to utilize the fruits of our labor.

Seven

The Attorney/ PI Relationship

The female attorney stood poised near the plaintiff's table, her professional manner reflected in her appearance and years of success echoed in the calm manner in which she took charge of the court room. Calmly, she lifted her gaze from a page she had been studying. This page was part of a thick binder she periodically referred to as she posed questions to the defendant. The defendant visibly steadied himself for the questions to follow. Nerves solicited involuntary reactions from his hands and feet, a veil of perspiration glistened on his forehead, and a look of dread crossed his face, as the words began to roll off of the composed and commanding attorney's tongue.

Hiring a competent private investigator can be just as important as hiring a competent attorney. In any type of case, finding an attorney who enlists the services of a private investigator may mean the success of your suit. This is sometimes tough because many attorneys enlist the services of a private investigator, however, their knowledge of "how to use the information" to win a case may be limited. Probing into the lives and lifestyles of an opposing party may generally be out of the realm of an attorney's contractual obligation; therefore, finding an attorney who knows how to use the PI's information, is definitely in your best interest.

When you reach the point in your relationship where it becomes necessary to seek the advice of an attorney, you should look for an attorney who is familiar with the services of a private investigator. More importantly, find an attorney who knows how to use information obtained by the private investigator. You should consider that your attorney, regardless of his or her qualifications, needs all the information possible to properly represent you in this type of case. An attorney's information may be limited to documents that can be discovered through subpoena and or through discovery, whereas a private investigator may obtain many other details that, if not used as evidence in the trial, may be used by your attorney for intelligence purposes. Many times, it will give the attorney inside information unknown through the normal course of discovery and subpoena. This may result in your attorney having a great deal more leverage and bargaining power in resolving the case to your advantage.

Remember, it may be important to have an attorney that hires a private investigator, but it is more important to hire an attorney that knows how to properly utilize the information obtained by the private investigator. Our agency, having worked for numerous attorneys throughout the United States, may be able to assist by referring you to an attorney who knows the proper method of using various pieces of information obtained by the investigators.

It is not unusual for an individual, when telling his, or her, side of a story to tell only that which they want to make known. Whether you are the plaintiff or defendant, some witnesses will not always tell the whole truth, until confronted with facts to the contrary. In a divorce or custody battle, the less than truthful party may be even less forthcoming. This makes the work of a private investigator invaluable. Any party needing to develop a solid case should hire an investigator. A competent investigator will be knowledgeable in gathering specific information the attorney may not get through discovery or by a subpoena. Even then, many of these answers may only come back partially answered or after costly motions to comply. For the best possible results, find an attorney who engages the services of private investigators and, knows how to use the information gathered to better serve your case.

Consider the story of the older man first mentioned in chapter three. The PI picked up the discarded and abandoned items left curbside at the paramour's residence. When sorted and copied, it initially appeared that very little damaging information had been obtained; however, it was all filed into the attorney's binder. Originally unnoticed, there was included in this binder a "blank" page from a notepad with the name of an upscale resort hotel. When first discovered, the PI didn't realize how important this "blank" page from the notepad would prove to be. As the case got closer to trial, the client's attorney began to carefully review the information binder.

The investigation continued for several months, with the investigator getting visual information of the affair, as well as incriminating "proof" of the misuse of marital assets. The completed investigation was compiled for the attorney, including the paramour's history, photographs and a copy of items that had been discarded at the address of the paramour. Our client moved out of the marital residence and filed for divorce. Our client's attorney then scheduled a deposition of the client's husband for ten o'clock on a morning two months later. Based on the information documented by the PI, the attorney knew this time of day would be difficult for the subject because his body would need a drink soon, thus, a prime time for the deposition.

The deposition began, as all depositions begin, by establishing the identity of the person being deposed. The attorney, experienced and poised, coolly asked if the subject had a girlfriend, which the subject adamantly denied. He also denied even *knowing* the particular woman when he was asked about her by name. The attorney casually reminded him he was under oath and of the penalties involved with perjury. The questions continued as to whether he knew or had any knowledge of this woman. He finally admitted to *perhaps* knowing, or having heard of her, as being a former employee of a company he had sold some years ago.

The attorney then opened the thick information binder. He flipped to a page containing a photograph of the subject's vehicle and asked if he owned the vehicle, with the specific tag number, as shown in the photograph. At this time, the subject's attorney requested a break. After the break, his attorney stated his client would like to *rephrase* some of his answers to certain previous questions. To each question, he only affirmed a vague knowledge of the woman in question; however, admitted the vehicle in the photographs was indeed his.

Our client's attorney continued questioning the nature of the relationship between him and this woman. Had he purchased gifts for her? Was the relationship of a sexual nature? To which he continued to deny. Again, our client's attorney opened the binder and showed him a photograph of his vehicle pulling into the woman's garage and asked him to again, confirm this to be his vehicle. The subject began perspiring profusely. He continued to deny using any marital assets to pursue this woman. Again, the attorney opened the information binder and turned to a page containing a copy of a *resort hotel* memo pad, which was blank, yes, blank, of everything *except the identity of the resort hotel.*

Our client's spouse, because of the impact of the previous photographs of his vehicle, began to show signs of needing his morning alcohol fix. The attorney's pattern of showing a photograph, after asking questions led the subject to believe the attorney was looking at "real information" linking him to the resort hotel.

The attorney then asked, "Isn't it true Mr. So-and-So that you have, in fact, taken this woman to the so-and-so resort hotel?

The subject's attorney quickly asked for a ten-minute recess. He returned, and again the defendant's attorney advised that his client would like to rephrase some of his answers.

With this, the subject began admitting to having an intimate, long-term relationship with this woman, traveling the world with her and taking care of her financially. This included paying for her residence, vehicle and tuition at a local university.

When the case went to court the attorney was able to properly utilize information obtained by the private investigator and received a much higher settlement for the client. The attorney also knew how to use the information to the advantage of the client's case. This is just another example of how the work of a private investigator can compliment a case when combined with the efforts of a competent attorney.

There are no "typical" cases, just as there are no "typical" days in the life of a private investigator. Though many elements are the same, each case is new and distinctive. Each case is handled with a personal approach, while drawing upon our years of experience. Although this may be a new and even frightening situation for you, rest assured, someone with experience in these matters is in your corner, should you need us.

After agreeing to accept a case and having reviewed all the *intake sheet* information, we will meet with our investigator(s) and office staff to discuss who will be involved in putting the investigative puzzle together. The client's "believed to be facts" are reviewed and discussed. Almost, without exception, the investigators' minds begin showing what only years of experience will teach you. One by one, we see certain flaws, discrepancies and contradictions, and realize our client's facts are probably more lies than truth.

Once our internal office meeting is completed, a preliminary plan of action is determined and the investigation begins. From there on, God only knows what the picture will be when all the pieces of the puzzle are finally in place.

We endeavor to never forget the potential anguish and pain our client may feel when it comes time to make that, "Hello, Mr. or Mrs. Client, this is Mr. Adair. I would like to set up a time to meet with you and/or your attorney to review the information we have put together."

Eight

Conclusion

Behind dark windows he sat, using state-of-the-art video equipment to capture information. Several cameras, both video and still, adorn the passenger seat, some equipped with infrared devices, others with telescopic lenses, all conducive to this covert business. In his shirt pocket a tiny voice-activated tape recorder resides, primarily used to record his observation of who, what, when and where. His cell phone silently alerts him to a call.

In his customary quiet voice, he converses with someone, never taking his eyes off the location of his subject, while continually noticing everything going on around him. Patience is pushed to the maximum, but the investigator remains calm.

The only thing typical about a day in the life of a private investigator is, hopefully, waking up in the morning and returning to bed at night (unless I'm working a case, which is almost every night). Other than that, there is nothing typical about a day in the life of a private investigator.

I try to get to my office at least once every day, unless I am out of town investigating a case. Countless days I have left my residence, headed for the office and ended up on a plane to somewhere halfway across the country and many miles away from my office. I recall one particular occasion; I had asked my adult daughter out to breakfast and to ride with me to the gas station. We ended up in another state. My daughter now thinks twice before she goes with me to breakfast or to run errands.

One afternoon, while watching a subject at his place of business, I noted there was nothing out of the ordinary going on. Suddenly, the subject left his office. Based on his erratic work schedule, leaving at different times during the afternoon and then returning, this was not unusual. I kept the subject under traveling surveillance, assuming he would make his usual stops before heading home or back to his office. Was I in for a surprise? Within minutes, we had merged onto the southbound lane of an Interstate Highway. We continued southbound for 225 miles before exiting at an upscale hotel in Dallas, Texas. The surprises continued, as later that night I found myself in an even more surprising situation.

After settling into the beautiful upscale hotel, the subject left the hotel only to drive about two blocks to a nearby *'hard-core' Gentleman's Club.* Here he met another male in the bookstore portion of the Club. After a brief exchange of words, they entered the movie theatre section. There they enjoyed a movie only men relieving each other's sexual fantasies would enjoy. My covert camera with night vision lens neatly tucked away in a gym bag captured everything, leaving nothing to the imagination.

The next day, I was in for another surprise. After returning to the hotel, the subject went directly to his room. I then casually asked a clerk at the front desk what time my friend in room number 306 wanted his wakeup call, as I needed to get up forty-five minutes earlier to go get gas. Of course, the desk clerk, wanting to help, set my wake-up call forty-five minutes prior to the subject's. I needed to be in the car and waiting as the subject exited the hotel.

When the subject came out of the hotel, he loaded his clothes and left with me in close pursuit. I had no idea where we were going next. Some 350 miles later, I covertly followed the subject to another upscale hotel, this time in Tunica, Mississippi, the casino capital of the Midwest.

Here, I watched the subject lose a few thousand dollars of marital assets. Not only did I get extraordinary video and documentation of his extramarital activities, I also acquired a nice bonus in the process. While intensely focused on the subject's gambling, I discreetly sat downat a dollar slot machine, unconsciously depositing my three, one-dollar tokens into the machine. Imagine my shock to find, that on the third pull of the lever, my cash flow was increased by $5,000!

In view of the fact that there is really no typical day in a private investigator's life, most investigators are prepared to travel anywhere, at any moment, which means maintaining:

- A valid passport.
- A bag packed in the vehicle for seven days/nights of travel.
- Seven days of required daily medications, if applicable.
- Enough cash to take care of certain incidentals and an ATM card.
- Credit card for air travel, rental car and lodging.

In addition, all of the investigator's tools-of-the-trade must be readily accessible at all times, including binoculars, cameras, extra batteries, battery and equipment chargers, plenty of film and/or memory sticks and a large allocation of patience.

We never know what strange places or where the day might take us; such as the morning I headed in the direction of my office only to end up walking off of the plane in Costa Rica twelve hours later. Fortunately, everything was packed. All I had to do was grab my bags and catch the flight.

On another less-than-typical day, I was retained by a very dependent, stay-at-home mother to investigate the activities of her husband, to whom she had been married for twenty-six years. The client's spouse, a physician, announced, this particular morning, he would be speaking at a "medical conference" in the west Texas town of Amarillo. Surveillance began around 10:15 a.m. in Edmond, Oklahoma.

The subject left his residence at 11:05 a.m. After following him running about town, taking care of his errands, we ended up some three hours later at a Hampton Inn in Tulsa for the night. The next day, we got an early start leaving the hotel, and a few hours later, I found myself on a riverboat casino in Kansas City, Missouri, watching the subject entertain a lovely lady, who was approximately twenty years younger than he.

The next day the couple spent a quiet morning together, having breakfast on the veranda of the woman's upscale home. In the evening our subject and his paramour dined on steak and lobster at one of the best steak houses in Kansas City. The next morning I followed the subject back into the arms of his wife and children.

It is quite typical to begin my day in one state and end up in another. Following a subject into their maze of illicit betrayal, infidelity and deceit is also quite typical.

Uncertainty is the only thing predictable about the profession of a private investigator. We never know where the trail is going to lead, twist, turn, double back or dead-end. We just follow the lead and find ourselves waltzing across town or even the country. Good instinct and intuition are necessary, but a good investigator must keep an open mind and a neutral disposition, in order to successfully use his inherent skills, knowledge and experience.

This is a fleeting look into the hectic job and whirlwind life of a private investigator. I hope after reading this book you will feel more comfortable about enlisting the assistance of a competent private investigator, should you ever need one.

If nothing else, perhaps this book will positively affect the manner in which you interact with your spouse or significant other. When a spouse, or significant other, observes or is exposed to deceitful behavior, it strikes a cord within us to put forth an attempt to relate and respond to our partners with extra care and caution. This applies to oneself, as well. No one likes to see him/herself reflected in a mirror where betrayal is revealed.

I hope you never need our services, however, if, and when, you do, we are here to FIND OUT THE TRUTH. May God bless you and your marital relationship.

END NOTES

[1]Geringer, Joseph . "Allan Pinkerton and His Detective Agency: "We Never Sleep" Roots of a Detective." Crime Library. Court TV's Crime Library. 05 07 2004 <http://www.crimelibrary. com/ gangsters_outlaws/cops_others/pinkerton/1.html?sect=1.

[2]Geringer, Joseph . "Allan Pinkerton and His Detective Agency: "We Never Sleep". A Tradition is Born" Crime Library. Court TV's Crime Library. 05 07 2004 <http://www.crimelibrary. com/gangsters_ outlaws/cops_others/pinkerton/2.html?ect=2>.

[3]"Private Detectives and Investigators." Occupational Outlook Handbook. U.S. Department of Labor: Bureau of Labor Statistics. 26 May. 2004 http://www.stats.bls.gove/oco/ocos157. htm>.

[4]"Safety Belts and Teens 2003 Report." National Highway Traffic Safety Administration. U.S. Department of Transportation.10 09 2004<http://www.nhtsa.dot.gov/people/injury/airbags/ buasbteens03/>.

[5]"Graduated Driver Licensing." National Highway Traffic Safety Administration. U.S. Department of Transportation. 10 09 2004 <http://www.nhtsa.dot.gov/PEOPLE/injury/New-fact-sheet03/ GraduatedDriver.pdf>.

[6]"Is Divorce the Answer for You?." Oklahoma Bar Association pamphlet September 2002: .

[7]"Table 3. Provisional number of marriages and divorces: Each State, December 2002 and 2003, and cumulative figures,2001-2003." National Vital Statistics Reports. 10 2004. Centers for Disease Control.19 May 2005http://www.cdc.gov/nchs/fastats/ divorce.htm>.

[8]"Mariage and Divorce." National Center for Health Statistics. 2003.CentersforDiseaseControl.19May2005 http://www.cdc.gov/ nchs/ fastats/divorce.htm>.

[9] Oklahoma Bar Association pamphlet September 2002

[10] Langer, Gary."Primetime Live." Primetime Live Poll: American Sex Survey: A Peek Beneath the Sheets. ABC News, New York City. 22 Oct 2004. Transcript. 09 11 2004 http://abcnews. go.com/Primetime/Print?id=156921>.

[11]"20/20 ." Sex: Myths, Lies and Straight Talk. ABC News, New York City. 05 Nov 2004. Transcript. 09 11 2004 <http://abcnews. go.com/2020/story?id=230011&page=2>.

[12]Vaughan, Peggy. "Office Affairs." Dear Peggy.com. Beyond Affairs Network. 22 03 2005 <http://www.dearpeggy.com/ articles.html>.

[13]Gertler, Stephanie. "To Love, Honor, and Betray." ABC News - Good Morning America. 04 2005. 22 03 2005 <http:// abcnews. go.com/GMA/print? id=464266>.

[14]"Child Custody, Divorced Families, 1997." Children's Rights Council. National Center for Health Statistics. 23 08 2004 <http:// gocrc.com/research/spgrowth.html>.

[15]"Joint Custody and Shared Parenting: What the Research Says, What Parents Say." Children's Rights Council. Children's Rights Council. 28 05 2004 <http://gocrc.com/research.html>.

[16]"Parenting as a Fundamental Right." Children's Rights Council. Children's Rights Council. 23 08 2004 <http://www.gocrc.com/constitution.html>.

[17] Sherr, Lynn. "Shadowy Addiciton." ABC NEWS. 27 2004. ABC News 20/20. 01 09 2004 <.htmlhttp://www.abcnews.go.com/sections/2020/scitech/2020_cyberporn_040827.html>.

ABOUT THE AUTHOR

M. DUANE ADAIR learned at an early age he had a passion for investigating people's elusive lifestyles, activities and habits believed by the perpetrator to be known only by him. Mr. Adair began his investigating career working for the Federal Bureau of Investigation in Washington, D.C. While working at the FBI, he attended George Washington University in Georgetown, MD, followed by attending West Texas A and M University, Canyon, Texas. After a period of time in the real estate and oil business, in 1980 Mr. Adair initiated his vision of forming his own private investigating agency. Adair and Associates was successfully developed into one of the most successful private investigation agencies in the region. The agency concentrates on being diligent, meticulous and persistent with a commitment to finding out the truth.

When Mr. Adair is not personally in the field investigating a case, you will find him busy sharing his experiences with audiences throughout the United States.

TONYA KILBURN is a free-lance writer and dance artist. Her work has appeared in various local art journals and theatrical works. She specializes in curriculum writing and has authored training manuals and technical forms. Tonya holds a BFA from the University of Oklahoma and is currently studying professional education at the University of Central Oklahoma. She works as an Artist-in-Residence through the State Arts Council, is Associate Artistic Director for Prairie Dance Theatre and has been employed as a writer for Adair and Associates since 2003.

ABOUT THE ARTIST

BENJI PECK (Cover Design) grew up in Houston, TX, later moving to Oklahoma City, OK, where he attended a private university studying graphic design, advertising and illustration. After completing his studies, Mr. Peck began his career with a design studio in Oklahoma City, concepting and designing websites and identity design.

After two years at Visual Inventor, a new challenge found him in Nashville, TN designing CD and record labels. He jumped at the opportunity to combine his two passions, music and design. While in Nashville, Benji realized the more he knew about the client, the more personal and connecting the results. With this realization, he started B POSI+IVE INC., a full-service design studio. B POSI+IVE INC. came from Benji's aspirations to make design more personal. Concept-driven design giving personal appreciation to the client has resulted in B POSI+IVE INC. becoming a leading design boutique with marketing savvy.

ROBERT WOOD (Interior Artwork) found art to be a pleasing past time from an early age. He attended school all across America with a family always on the move. Robert studied two-dimensional art in college becoming practiced in several styles and mediums. As the oldest of five children, he has learned the value of communication and has continued to have a passion for visual art. Currently, Robert works as a mural painter for one of the prestigious groups working consistently throughout the region, and has several high profile jobs under his belt, as well as, a busy muralist, he participates in shows and takes commissions for personal work. Robert spends what free time he can with those that motivate his work the most, his family, good friends, and significant other.

Lightning Source UK Ltd.
Milton Keynes UK
18 December 2009

147691UK00001BA/125/A

9 781420 865417